# Come Day,
## Go Day,
## God Send
## Sunday

# The Singing of John Maguire

There is an LP record of John Maguire singing
some of the songs found between these covers.
The record, produced by Robin Morton, has
been released by Leader Records, 5 North Villas,
London NW1.

We look on the book and record as
complementary to one another, and we hope
that contact with one will lead you to consult
the other. This will surely expand your
enjoyment of this half of the combined effort.
More important it is hoped that it will increase
your appreciation of the songs and singing of
John Maguire.

♣♣♣

John Maguire feeding his pigs

# Come Day, Go Day, God Send Sunday

*The songs and life story,*
*told in his own words, of John Maguire,*
*traditional singer and farmer*
*from Co. Fermanagh*

*Collated by*

Robin Morton

Routledge & Kegan Paul   London

*First published in 1973*
*by Routledge & Kegan Paul Ltd,*
*Broadway House, 68–74 Carter Lane,*
*London EC4V 5EL*
*Printed in Great Britain by*
*Cox & Wyman Ltd,*
*London, Fakenham and Reading*

*ISBN 0 7100 7634 7*

'For une paysanne'

# Contents

# Plates

# Introduction

Experts have for years been warning us that, as a living tradition, the folk music and song of Ireland is fast dying. While not wishing to assist any complacency it must be said that this pessimism simply does not seem to coincide with the facts. The 'tradition' seems alive and well – perhaps as a result of well-timed warnings, who knows? Look at the number of good young pipers, fiddlers, flute players, etc.; and there are any number of fine young singers who are experiencing and sharing much delight in the 'old songs'. Perhaps they are changing things a little but then change is of the essence. An unchanging tradition is surely a dead one, and thus of interest only to the antiquarian.

Not only has this 'revival' of interest led the young people to sing and play traditional music, but many of the older generation have taken down forgotten fiddles, or are remembering songs they used to sing. For those who never stopped practising their art there is a new and keen audience wanting to know how it used to be played and sung. The province of Ulster seems to be particularly well endowed with these carriers of the old tunes and songs. This endowment, with a few notable exceptions, has been largely ignored by the scholars and collectors. More recently, however, some have remarked, with ill-concealed amazement, on the strength of the tradition in that province, especially that of song. This is the story of one of the carriers of that song tradition.

I first met John Maguire on a Sunday in late September 1968 and I am now pleased to number him and his wife and family among my friends. However it was because of his reported competence as a singer that I first went to see him in the company of the late Paddy McMahon. It was Paddy, himself a fine, strong singer, who told me about John. So one Sunday afternoon, and armed with a dozen Guinness, we knocked on the door of the cottage at Tonaydrumallard, near Rosslea in Co. Fermanagh. We were ushered into a small, tidy farm kitchen and formal introductions were made. We were lucky to get John there at all, we were told. That day he had just come out of hospital after a car accident, and an injury to his neck was still paining him.

John was sitting on a large leather armchair, in the corner under the American wall-clock, and he looked in obvious discomfort as a result of the accident. I was sure there would be no singing that day but as the afternoon passed we all relaxed and the crack got better. Paddy sang a couple of songs and I held up my end. Then Paddy, always a marvellous catalyst, wondered if John remembered the song about Lough Ooney (see song 24, chapter 5). John thought maybe he would if he could 'just get into the start of it'. Well get into the start of it he did and before we left that evening John had given me about twelve songs and an assurance that I would be welcome back any time. I have returned often.

Here is a man who not only has good songs but sings them in a way that shows much of what is best in the 'Ulster style' of traditional singing. In this we do not find the vocal gymnastics of the 'sean nos' singing of the west. The decorations used by John are subtle – they have to be listened for, but they are no less effective because of that. The story is all important and nothing is allowed to cloud that. John Maguire is first and foremost a story-teller. His timing is uncanny and the word that springs to mind when attempting to pinpoint the essence of his style is 'economy'.

John Blacking, an ethnomusicologist and Professor of Social Anthropology at Queen's University, Belfast, has lent his skills to transcribing John's singing into musical form. Many thanks are due to him for this invaluable contribution. While the task was no doubt a difficult one, it seems also to have held much fascination. Thus we can look forward to a fuller analysis from Professor Blacking when, freed from the pressure of publication dates, etc., he has had time to work over the material. In the interim he explains his method of transcription in the note on p. 97.

Other aspects of the songs, it is hoped, have been dealt with in appendix 4 where it has been attempted to place them within a social and historical context, in so far as that is relevant. The project might have ended there – another folk-song collection to add to those already available. However something more has been attempted here.

I have been 'collecting' folksongs for a number of years now and slowly but surely it has dawned on me that a song alone is a fairly isolated thing. Some may be minor works of art but decisions about what is, and what is not, art is a very personal matter. What one person sees as 'good' might very well be called 'bad' by his neighbour. Perhaps then it is as part of the past that I am interested in folksongs – a sort of musical word transparency that offers the historian new insights. Here we might find the thoughts and emotions of the 'ordinary people'. By them the details of everyday life, which do much to clothe bare history, are highlighted. Jan Vansina has suggested that 'comparison of oral sources with other kinds of historical source is a little like juxtaposing and superimposing a number of photographs with and upon the other, so that a larger area of landscape can be seen, and seen more clearly' (*Oral Tradition*, translated by H. M. Wright, Routledge & Kegan Paul, 1965, p. 142).

The opinion grew in me that it is *in* the singer that the song becomes relevant. Analysing it in terms of motif, or rhyming structure, or minute variation becomes, in my view, sterile if the one who carries the particular song is forgotten. We have all met the scholar who can talk for hours in a very learned fashion about folksong and folklore in general, without once mentioning the singer. Bad enough to forget the social context, but to ignore the individual context castrates the song. As I got to know the singers so I got to know and understand their songs more fully. No longer had I to wonder about relevance because once I knew the people who were singing to me relevance became a self-conscious irrelevancy. The relevance was in Davy Menish, or Tom Todd, or Tommy Gunn, or in this case John Maguire.

Of all the singers I have met I came to know John best of all. In some way he struck a chord in me; I wanted to know *him* as well as his songs. Questions began to form in my mind – Why did he sing the songs that he sang? Indeed why did he sing at all? I often asked John, but he never really could answer, in fact I sometimes wonder if such questions had any meaning for him at all. Slowly it dawned on me that I was not asking the right questions. Now I know about John and his life I think I know the answers to my original questions without really having asked them. Had I tried I could have put these answers into some form. I have not attempted to do this however. To do so would have meant editing out much of John's story and this, after all, is *his* story. Also I hope that you will have your own questions to ask and that the story that follows will help you to answer them, whether you be musicologist, folklorist, anthropologist, historian or simply a general reader.

In this volume will be found John's full repertoire of songs. Probably by the time this is published he will have come up with a few more; but at the end of 1971 these are the songs and fragments of songs, that he had given me. Two-thirds are contained in the main text and the rest are tacked on in an appendix. The story itself is in John's own words, as told into my tape-recorder in late 1970. I filled seven tapes and then edited the material in order to give some shape to the story line. I can feel some readers nodding knowingly and I understand their misgivings when they read words such as 'editing'. So let me attempt to allay some of these fears by explaining my methods.

First of all I knew John very well before I ever started this project. I discussed with him what I wanted to do and he agreed to 'have a go'. So we sat down with an empty tape on the recorder and began. I first asked a very general question – 'Tell me about your early life.' I always asked general questions except when I wanted something explained in more detail. Once I had asked a question I sat quietly and let John talk. Even when he seemed to have finished I sat with an expectant look in the hope that he would continue, as he often did. Only when he seemed to have nothing more to say did I continue with a subsidiary query, or go on to a new area altogether. To the extent that I asked questions at all the 'story' probably tells as much about me and my interests as it does about John. It is difficult to see how one sidesteps such a danger completely. However I must ask you to accept that I was continually ready to respond to 'hints' from John as to what areas we should discuss, and often I left it up to him to decide what we should talk about next. I would also suggest that the fact that I know John very well was an important corrective in keeping the influence of my personal 'hobby-horses' to a minimum.

This factor was also useful in editing the tapes. To translate these straight on to paper would have been confusing, to say the least. We jumped about from pillar to post, one minute talking about the day he crashed the doctor's car (chapter 2) and then of a recent trip to 'jandies well' (chapter 5). So if the story was to be published it would have to be put into some shape, some pattern. What I did then was to gather all the material together, in approximately chronological order, and then join the lot up in such a way as to make it flow. In doing so I took care not to interfere overly with John's syntax.

Some conventions in translation from speech to the written word have been used and should be noted. For instance where a word is constantly pronounced in a colloquial way then I have used the word that is most often written, e.g. the word old is pronounced 'ould' but I have used *old* in the text. Had this not been done the result would have been complicated phonetic spellings which would have often been impossible to read. Once the convention had been decided upon it was always used even in the case of obvious words like 'ould'. Where words were given a peculiar pronunciation, a phonetic spelling has been attempted, e.g. 'browncatis' for bronchitis. Where a word is pronounced in two ways interchangeably I have given these as used, e.g. his and he's. As far as the songs are concerned I have given them exactly as John sang them to me. Sometimes there were words that did not seem to fit into the story line. In these cases I have given the original words and immediately after the incongruity I have suggested an alternative, enclosed in brackets. The words italicized in the text are words that it is felt need fuller explanation. A glossary for each chapter will be found at the end of the book. It should be noticed that once a word has been included in the glossary it is assumed that it is not necessary to deal with it again.

Some readers may find fault in my methods – that is their right and privilege – but at least I have offered them for inspection. Perhaps the fact that I am at least aware of the intrinsic problems in such a project may answer some fears regarding the 'objectivity' of the result.

May I finally take this opportunity to express my gratitude to some of the many people who have helped in various ways to develop the idea into a reality. John Blacking has already been thanked for his much appreciated assistance. Thanks are also due to Margaret Arthur for the photographs and to the Ulster Folk Museum for permission to use W. A. Green's fine study of the poteen still. Celia Tobin, Beverly Witham and Evelyne McIntosh suffered much in typing the manuscript and Len Partridge gave invaluable aid in copying tapes for transcription purposes. I should like to mention Hamish Henderson and Pat Shuldham-Shaw and thank them for giving so freely of their wide knowledge of the traditional song of these islands. Mrs Mullarkey, a neighbour of John's, made the book more complete by allowing me to use her version of 'The Burning of Rosslea' (song 55). Thank you Elly. However the main burden of my appreciation must obviously go to Mr and Mrs John Maguire, not only for putting up with my endless questions but also for supplying some of the best tea I have ever had in my life.

ROBIN MORTON

# As the cocks they began to crow . . .

## Molly Bawn Lowry

Come all you late fowlers that carry a gun,
Beware of late fowling in the dark of the sun;
Beware of late fowling, when what happened of late,
It was Molly Bawn Lowry and a-hard was her fate,

She being coming from her uncle's, when a shower came on,
Went under a green bush the shower to shun;
With her apron all round her, I took her for a swan
But to my misfortune I shot Molly Bawn.

I stepped up to her with my gun in my hand,
My limbs they grew feeble and my eyes could not stand.
I wiped her fair temples till I found she was dead
And a fountain of tears for my darling I shed.

I ran home 'til my father with my gun in my hand
Saying, 'Father, dear father, do you know what I've done?
I shot Molly Bawn Lowry the pride of Athlone,
That lovely wee lassie I intended my own.'

She being coming from her uncle's when a shower came on
She went under a green bush, the shower to shun.
With her apron all round her I took her for a swan,
But to my misfortune I shot Molly Bawn.

Out bespoke my old father, his old locks were grey,
'Oh! son, dearest son, you do not go away.
Don't leave your own country till the assizes comes on,
You ne'er will be hanged for shooting a swan.'

Oh! the day of her funeral, it was a grand sight
To see four and twenty of them and all dressed in white;
Bore her on their shoulders, laid her in her clay;
They turned their backs and they all walked away.

But take four and twenty of them, put them all in a row,
And her beauty shines round them like a fountain of snow.

Now since it's decreed for that I was her doom,
That I was her butcher instead of her groom;
There is no other breathing that e'er I will take,
I will travel this world my soul for to make.

That was a song I got from my mother. She had a lot of songs you know. Had I learned half of them I wouldn't sing them for a whole day! Her name was Bridget McMahon *recently*, and she came from a place called Corbann, *a townland* not so far away from where we were reared. My father was Hugh Maguire and he came from Co. Armagh, near Markethill somewhere. To some *friends* of *he's* he came to at first, and stayed with them and bought a wee place.

My father died young. He took a bad pain down his leg and into his big toe. He didn't live very long altogether now when he took it. He was fifty-six or seven. It would be about fifty years ago, or just over it. I just remember him and nothing more; I think I was about ten or twelve years old. Of course I was the youngest and he died fairly sudden . . . Only I remember him singing. They were very jolly and he was a fair good singer and so was she. My father had a lot of old songs too. He used to be singing them at night when we'd be sitting round the fire, so I picked up this one that I was fairly interested in. It was about a boy that was born in America and he had Irish feelings. His father and mother both was Irish and he had great feelings for Ireland. I wouldn't be more than twelve or thirteen when I heard this, so this is the way it went on:

## Columbia the Free

Columbia the free, it's the land of my birth;
My pack is all over American earth.

2

My blood is as Irish as Irish can be,
And me heart's in green Erin far over the sea.

I have tops of green shamrock, I have sods they brought o'er;
I have shells that they picked up when leaving the shore;
I have books that I treasure, the fondest I hold
With their melody [metallic] clasp all nigh covered in gold.

I will sing their old songs, I will call them my own;
They are true to old Ireland in style or [and] in tone.
I will dance the dear dances and cheer them with glee;
Each touch are for Ireland far over the sea.

Oh if I was in beautiful Dublin today,
'Til that sainted old spot I would soon find my way.
I know where O'Connell and Curran are laid,
And beloved Robert Emmett sleeps cold in the shade.

Oh if I was in Wexford, it's fondly I'd trace,
Each field I would mark on my map of the place,
Where the brave '98 men poured, hotly and free,
Their blood for green Erin far over the sea.

Oh but land of my fathers I hold you to blame;
My cheeks do at times take acrimson with shame.
Has the sad tales not shone on that narrow stained line,
That the might of these tyrants were greater nor thine.

She has soldiers many abroad and at home;
Her ships on all oceans are ploughing the foam;
Her wealth are untold but no equal is she
For our poor plundered Ireland far over the sea.

Now I have a rifle that's true to a hair,
A brain that can plan, or a hand that can dare;
There summonses will scarce have died out when I'll be
On the green hills of Ireland far over the sea.

I didn't know any of the father's friends. They were all dead
before I came, but I remember my mother's side. There was
Peter McMahon. He lived in Corbann where he was reared, but
he had another place up about Clones at Duncrew, and he had a
place at Drumgross too. And *I mind* my Uncle Brian. He went

3

away to America when he was fairly young, but he came back again. I remember him telling a strange story about a comrade of he's from Clones. He was along with Uncle Brian and there was another man, drunk and wanting them to fight. This man that was along with my Uncle Brian struck him. So he fell and he hit the kerbstone with his head and it killed him. So my Uncle Brian went away to America a while after that. The other was brought down to Armagh and tried for murder, but the medical evidence of the doctor freed him. The bat on his head, on the kerbstone, killed him. It wasn't the man striking him at all, it wasn't that caused the death, so the medical give. So he wrote to Brian about going out to America, for he said he was annoyed in this country. No matter where he went this character that he struck at Clones was following him. Every night he went out he'd be walking alongside of him, so he thought he'd get rid of him if he was out there. He landed out with Brian, but it was nothing better if it wasn't worse. He was there too and walked alongside of him till the day he died.

I do believe at that time there was evil spirits because I have heard and knowed about the 'Cooneen Ghost', and I'm nearly perfectly sure that that was right. Several people I had been talking to went to that house and they knowed all about it. The first was knowed about it was when the children of the house used to be sleeping in school. The master used to beat them for it and then some of them, *when they got up middling*, were fit to tell that they were annoyed at night by 'the Ghost'. It used to pull the clothes off the children in bed and roll them out on to the floor. And even the man and woman could get no rest with it either, a terrible noise all the night through. So they went to America to get rid of it, but they say that it was just as bad on the ship going over, and in America too.

Then I mind an old man, he used to usually *ceilidh* to our house in my young days. He was always telling about ghost stories, about ghosts that people seen and what happened to them afterwards if they interfered with the spirit that appeared. He told about an old man, the name of Cassidy, who was coming home from a wee place called Corranay. He saw a man in front of him on the road and he thought to himself it was some individual man that was out like himself. So he passed no remarks till he came up close to him. He found out that he was a very big man. So he went to slip on by quietly but he wouldn't let him by. He moved in front of him from on one side of the road to the other, as hard as he could move. He was a very big, strong, able man. So he went to dash through this figure that was in front of him on the road, but he got a slap and he fell on the road. The next morning the people got him, he was terribly beaten. So he went to the hospital for a while, but he never got over it, it killed him.

The place where this happened was at a place where an old blacksmith at one time shoed horses and donkeys. There is nobody to this day likes to go past the forge. You see the people thinks the blacksmith is the ghost. He was a very heavy drinker and something happened to him at the forge, and he died over the head of it. At them times they said it was a mule or a jennet. He got a kick from it and he never got over it. They think to themselves that that was the cause of the evil spirit being out after that. Well I suppose them that's not at rest, or they have some purgatory to put in in this earth, are wandering about after they die. They don't get to heaven. I suppose there's some characters that bad that they might never get to heaven. There's no way to set them free I'm afraid, it's just the Man up above can do that.

There was a song that I used to hear my mother at – it was about ghosts – but I have only a bit of it:

> As Mary lay sleeping, her lover came creeping,
> To the bed chamber where she lay

Then there was a lot more that I can't mind and then:

## Willie's Ghost

> Oh Willie dear where are the blushes
> That you had some time ago?
> Oh Mary dear the cold clay changed them,
> For I'm the ghost of your Willie O.
>
> That night they spent in deep discoursing
> Of the courtships they had some time ago.
> They kissed, shook hands, with a sorrowful parting
> As the cocks they began to crow.

That's all I mind but you see it was *an old word* that when the cocks crew all ghosts was *off the pad*. You wouldn't meet a ghost then up above. I always heard that.

My mother lived to be over seventy years of age now. She was in fair form with a touch of *brownchatis* do you see. In fact I think *it bid be* that killed her at the latter end. It would be about thirty-three years ago. She always sung when she was in a wee spot of trouble. She'd just strike up a wee verse for us round the fireside. And if there gathered a few in, she would probably give them a song too and sometimes at a wedding party or anything like that. I remember her singing in the kitchen when there was *ceilidhers* in at night, and work was all done, she sung this song:

## Behind Yon Blue Mountain

Oh, behind yon blue mountain where the summit stands high,
I watched the sun rising so proud in the sky.
Where the great clouds were drifting and the sun-beams
  o'erthrown
O'er the high, lofty hills in the County Tyrone.

Fare ye well unto Clogher, likewise Fivemiletown,
Where we danced and played football with our comrades all
  around;
For singing or dancing her equal's unknown,
For these [this] charming wee lassies [lassie] that I met in
  Tyrone.

My poor heart is breaking with sorrow and pain
My friends and companions I'll ne'er see again.
Its lakes may go dry and its streams cease to moan
Before I forget of you lovely Tyrone.

Tomorrow I'm leaving the land of my birth,
I still think on thee as the fairest on earth,
I will pray for old Ireland, Sarsfield and Wolfe Tone
And behind me I'm leaving them hills of Tyrone.

Fare ye well unto Clogher, likewise Fivemiletown,
Where we danced and played football with our comrades all
  around,
For singing or dancing her equal's unknown,
For these charming wee lassies I met in Tyrone.

I remember my mother had hundreds of songs. I could have learned a whole lot of them but it's hard to think of them at the present time. But this is one I usually heard her singing:

## Lovely Jane from Enniskea

One evening fair in lovely June I carelessly did stray,
The fields with acclamation rang, and flowers decked each vale,
Fair and delightful was the scene, and one thing seemed more gay,
And that was Jane that's free from stain in lovely Enniskea.

The demesne walls I thus ascend and thus accosted Jane,
Said I, 'Fair maid pray condescend and heal your lovesick swain,
For I am deep in love with you, rely on what I say,
Oh do not chide, but be my bride, fair Jane of Enniskea.'

'Indeed young man I know you not, although you have my name,
It must have been that man told you, goes down by yonder stream.
It is no use, I loved a youth and single I will stay,
A maid I'll roam till he comes home through lovely Enniskea.'

'Oh yes it was that man goes down by yon stream told me your name, was Jane,
But from what you state I plainly see your favour I won't gain,
Come tell to me the lad you loved, and then I'll go away,
Ah the truth to tell he's Willie Bell that strayed from Enniskea.'

These last words took me by surprise, indeed I was the man,
That led me at once to know my charming Jane McCann.
The token was a golden ring, she gave when going away,
That I showed to Jane to prove her swain in lovely Enniskea.

When she saw the mark upon the ring she clasped her arms round me,
'Oh Willy dear it's ten long years since last I did you see,
You're welcome quite, my heart's delight home from Americay
Until your Jane that's free from stain in lovely Enniskea.'

7

Then slowly we did travel down by yon flowery vale,
To we reached her mama's cottage, lay near to Ravensvale,
We quickly published up our banns, got married without
    delay,
Me and my love were like two doves in lovely Enniskea.

I had three sisters and three brothers* and my oldest sister
married when she was about twenty-two. Her name was Mary
Ellen and she was married to a man named Patrick Gallagher.
They lived in Knocknagross where I live now. I wasn't too old
at the time, I just remember the wedding and nothing more. I
remember them talking about it. They had a great time and that,
and it was all side-cars and horses drawing them. There was no
motor-cars hardly.

She was a very nice person, very friendly and harmless. She was
between sixty-nine and seventy when she died. I'm thinking it's
up to twelve years ago now. She used to sing some songs too but
I don't remember much of them now. I'd have more of my
mother's songs because she was reared in that place at my uncle's
in Corbann you see, from she was very small and she wasn't so
much at home. Just at that time my aunts and uncles liked to
have some company. They hadn't married you see and she went
to stop with them when she was about seven or eight year old.
She was reared by her aunts and uncles, but all the rest of us were
reared at home.

Well anyway Biddy was next. She must be eighty years of age
now. She's always lived at Follom Big – that's the home place –
and so does Brian. He'd be about four or five years older *nor* me.
He was in Scotland but he wasn't long there altogether. He came
home and wrought on the farm. He got it when my mother died,
I'd say he'd have been in his thirties – thirty-two.

Brian and I used to sing a bit together. What they call an M.C.
would be conducting a place and asking certain people to sing.
So he used to ask the Maguires, both Maguires, me and Brian for
to sing. Both men and women sung together if they knowed the
song. Usually at that time they were used to it and could do it

* Chronological list of John's brothers and sisters:
Mary Ellen, b. 1892, d. 1958; Bridget (Biddy), b. 1893;
Margaret, b. 1895, d. 1939; Edward, b. 1896, d. 1964;
Brian, b. 1897; Patrick, b. 1900, d. 1953; John, b. 1902.

8

fairly well together; one could help the other. Sometimes a couple
would join in on the chorus only, but a lot of times they joined in
on the whole song – knowing it I suppose the same as the other
one did. And perhaps maybe he was a good singer and could sing
well along with them you see, had the same kind of voice and the
same way of *lowering it and rising it.*

There's one and I think Brian used to sing it along with me
now. That was one of Nelly's* songs, 'The Maid of Magheracloon'.

## The Maid of Magheracloon

You maidens all both great and small come listen unto me,
To I relate the dreadful state of my sad destiny.
I was courted by a fair young man and he has proved my
    ruin,
Which leaves me broken-hearted on the hills of Magheracloon.

He cares no more to meet me on a Sunday after Mass
Nor to listen 'til my footsteps when homewards I do pass,
Coming home from his night's rambling I do hear his merry
    tune
It reminds me of the time he came 'til the maid of
    Magheracloon.

Oh many's the pleasant hour I spent behind yon hawthorne
    tree
Telling tales of fond true love with innocence and glee.
Where is the hand that used to pull the blossoms in full bloom
And twine in the waving curls of the maid of Magheracloon.

He is not to blame, the fault's my own I really do confess;
And on a bed of sorrows I'll see my trouble's rest.
I will give my love to another young man both morning,
    night and noon,
Which leaves me broken-hearted on the hills of Magheracloon.

I was singing whenever I went to school first, in fact before I
went to school at all. You'll take an interest in some song or a
murder song or a comic or anything like that. If you take an

---

* Nelly Mullarky, a neighbour. See *Folksongs Sung in Ulster*,
Mercier Press, 1970, song 21.

interest in it you'll learn it. The story's important; at them times it was very important. It was like somebody emigrating to America and a song made about them or something like that. The people all round about here was interested in them things, in emigration and love songs and one thing and another. I'd have a lot more songs if I minded them but sure you'd forget a lot of them. I'd have bits of them, it would be like what Patrick* said about the songs, 'Everyone had a bit of it and no one had it all.' He used to be always saying that.

The air's very important too, the tune that will be 'til that, is very important because there be's lovely airs 'til songs and that makes the song very interesting. The way the air can be turned and lowered and ris, that was a very good thing in our young days. They'd tell you about how much a man could turn a song, like raise it and lower, and the way their voices could change a lot. There was some very good singers you know about this country. If you knowed music you'd know he had an air to start with, and if you were fond of music you'll know it. Then a man that can use the words and pronounce them right, when he has a good air, he's a good singer.

I never was hard to learn that way, I could pick up a song if it was a couple of times sung for me and I'd pick up the air too. Many's the time there was songs wrote, I would learn on paper there you know, still if I heard them sung a couple of times I'd have them. There's a song there I'm after singing for you, that's the Maid of Magheracloon. I remember I heard Tom McQuillan singing in Rosslea Hall at a concert. That would be back in the 'twenties and there was a bit of the third verse there I hadn't it. But I was in Corraghy Hall and he was what they called an M.C. in it at that time, and he used to be giving out the dances and everything. And I asked him if he would sing this song for us and he says, 'If you call me out I'll sing it.' So he sung it for me and I had it all. That was only the twice I heard it. I'd remember the story and if I remembered the story you see it wasn't too hard to put in a word if you wanted, into it. Once you knowed the story of a song and the air of it you'd have very little trouble in carrying on. When I had it Brian had it too you see, because he wouldn't be too long picking it up either with me singing it. You'll remember

* The late Paddy McMahon, the man who introduced me to John, as mentioned in the Introduction.

the main parts of it and if you remember the main parts of it you'll remember the rest – you can make it.

Pat was next. No wait, I think maybe it was Maggie was next now. That's right Maggie was next. She always wrought on the farm 'til she was about forty-three or four years. She died, took very ill and died. It was supposed to be a growth at that time. She wasn't too long bad but for a period of about seven or eight months.

Then there was Edward of course. He was working on the farm until when he got up about twenty or twenty-two years of age he married. He went to Scotland to the coal mines in Blantyre. There wasn't much money to be made in our part of the country at that time. He wrought in them till twelve months before he died, but he come always on a holiday home, in the month of July. He was a stout strong fellow, was always in good health till the day he died. It appears it had been a heart attack he took. *It would like to be* six years ago, he was sixty-eight then.

Patrick then was about a couple of years older than me but he happened a very bad accident. He was in Clones with a horse and cart and when he was coming home there was a shop-man was talking to him. And he asked him to bring some small parcels, globes of lamps and some other small articles with him. So when he came out the road, it was only about a mile to where the border was and the Customs was there on the road. They searched him and the cart and got these things that there was some duty on. So they turned him round and brought him away to Newtownbutler to the Custom authorities there. So when he was passing over a bridge where the train ran under, they called it Brown's Bridge, the horse scared and bolted and it run away about half a mile up the road and *cooped* the cart, and the horse tramped on his back and on his arm both. So he was an invalid for the rest of his days nearly. The time it happened he wouldn't be passing twenty-two or three. He went on a stick for a while but I went with him to a doctor in Monaghan, he was the name of Doctor Hall. So he told me he could give him a bottle, he said, for to relieve him a bit for a time. But he'd never gain strength nor he'd never be fit to walk because the spinal cord was touched. The track of the horse's shoe, *the caulkers* of the shoe, was in his back when he examined him. That caused the spinal cord to be affected. So anyhow, till the day he died he had to be took in a chair from the room to the kitchen and it was a long tough job now. He'd be dead about fifteen or sixteen years now I'm sure. They give him all the treatment they could and he was taken to the hospital on several occasions. He even was in hospitals all over. He was down in the hospital here in Belfast and he was in Dublin and he was everywhere, to see if they could do nothing. Aye, it was a long tough job now. Biddy and Brian looked after him in the later days; they have always lived at Follom Big. It must be about four or five perch from the road, and of course in the early days it was thatched. It's now corrugated iron, and there was two rooms and a kitchen. There was a little loft put on it now later, but in the early days there was just the two rooms and what the usual thing was, the beds was built into the walls, wooden beds you know, closed in. They weren't like the beds now, they were closed in beds you know, all boarded out from the walls right round. The beds were all closed in that way you know, you could close the doors when you went in. Then my mother and father slept on what they call press beds. They were a long bed kept in the kitchen. There might be a couple of them in the kitchen at the time and you'll get them in places yet do you know. They folded up and you could sit on them in a corner as a seat you see.

There was an open fire, a turf fire, and all was cooked on that open fire now. The main food that the people took at that time was potatoes and porridge. There was plenty of oaten meal, some bread and tea. All was cooked on the open fire and they baked cakes in ovens, put live coals on top and a fire in under do you see. Mrs Mullarky has the same style yet in making them. We got meat too of course, but it was seldom that they ever bought much beef at that time you know. There'd be fowl, cock chickens and turkeys and things like that, but very little flesh meat was bought, excepting what they produced at home. You would have it maybe once or twice a week. There might be a turkey or a goose or duck or a cock chicken. In the morning you'd have tea and you might have a boiled egg and butter. At that time they *churned* their own butter at home in what they called a churn. Sometimes if you cared for it or had a taste for it you'd take sometimes eggs and bacon. The pig would be killed. We'll say a heavy pig would be killed there that was overweight, and you'd get that cured and keep it in the house. It was very nice bacon, you couldn't get better, the pig you cured at home yourself.

In the middle of the day, one o'clock or thereabouts, if you wished you could have bacon and you might have cabbage, and if you wished to take eggs you could take them too. At night you'd have nearly always the oaten porridge and milk. You'd have potatoes only at dinner-time. They used to be what they called Champions. They were a very dry, good *pratie*. They were the best spuds to be got at that time till Kerrs Pinks come, it was a good pratie too. Many's the time you'd have potatoes on their own. You'd take milk and potatoes just and a bit of butter. It was churned with a churning staff and it might take three-quarters of an hour to churn it. You had to churn constant till you got it done. Well everyone took a hand at it. It was first left lie in crocks, crockery crocks, to it got leave to sour and get into a thick liver, a cream. Then it was put in the churn. After a week in them crocks put some warm water in it and you churned it and that's what they took the butter off.

# Here's a health to Tommy Kelly . . .

I would be about seven when I went to school. I had plenty of company from round about. Of course the rest of our ones was stopped school, excepting Patrick. He was with me for a while till he stopped school then about a year or two after that. You weren't asked to do too much the first while, you got a book and a pencil and you scribbled away on it. The mistress might come round after lunch-time and make a few letters for you to imitate them and so on. Every day she'd be making another few. You worked on that way, till you got to be fit to make all the letters.

There were two teachers in it do you see. There was a mistress and master both. The small ones was with the mistress, when they come to school first, learning their letters. Then when you got on to second and third class you went to the master. The master at my time was Master Burke, he was from County Sligo. Well we had several mistresses, we had Miss Harron and Miss Connolly, I was with them two. They were very nice now, very nice teachers, very good with children too but Master Burke was cross, a cross master. If you weren't reading right or writing or anything like that you'd get the tip of a pointer, what he used to point to the blackboard you know. He'd hit you about the head with it, or anywhere and he might slap you with it too. He had canes too of course. We used to steal the canes on him and slip them in under the wooden floor when we'd get him out. Ah! it was hard at that time. There was none of us liked school anyway. We learned what they called grammar and geography and Euclid and ordinary reading books. I might be able to call to memory some of the poems or something that was in the books.*

* 'The Burial of Sir John Moore', Charles Wolfe (1791–1823).

Not a drum was heard, not a funeral note
As the corpse to the ramparts we hurried,
Not a soldier discharged his farewell shot
O'er the grave where our hero we buried.
We buried him darkly at dead of night
The sods with our bayonets turning,
And the struggling moonbeam's misty light
And the lantern dimly burning.
No useless coffin enclosed his breast,
Not in sheet or in shroud we wound him,
He lay like a warrior taking his rest,
With his martial cloak around him.
Few and short were the prayers we said,
We spoke not a word of sorrow,
But steadfastly gazed on the face that was dead
And bitterly thought of the morrow.
We thought, as we hollowed his narrow bed
And smoothed down his lonely pillow,
That the foe and the stranger would tread over his
   head
And we far away on the billow.
Lightly they'll talk of the spirits that's gone
And over his cold ashes upbraid him;
But little he'll reck, if they'll let him sleep
In a place where a Briton has laid him.
When half of our heavy task was done,
The clock struck the note for retiring,
We heard in the distance and random gun
That the foe was sullenly firing.
Slowly and sadly we laid him down
From the field of his fame fresh and gory,
We carved not a line, nor we raised not a stone,
But we left him alone with his glory.

And then it was wrote at the foot of it the Reverend Charles Wolfe.
It was him that composed the poem.

There would be an odd boy sung about school but there were
very few at that time. They'd be very simple wee songs at school
at that time like:

## The Pony Song

Let the pony go fast as e'er it will,
Dobbin sure you know when he reached a hill.
What a merry ride, how we jog along,
See how snugly side by side and joining in a song.
    Jinkle bells, jinkle bells, jinkle all the way,
    Oh the funny ride we had down by Enniskea.

The schools was just the old national schools long ago. I see plenty of them there yet but they don't take school in them, they're gone 'til other jobs. There used to be several roofs here and there. You know, angled this way right and angled left. They're not the same built as the schools is built now you know. They had an ordinary fire of turf. You brought we'll say a load of turf and every child brought a load of turf to the school. They were drew on donkeys at that time, and creels. You had to buy your books and *copies* and things like that.

For a long time school started at half past nine, then it went to ten o'clock. You had to be in at ten o'clock and finished at four, sometimes it would be half past four when you'd get out. There wasn't free meals at that time. Whatever bread you brought with you in your school-bag you ate it at twelve o'clock when you got out to play.

I mind this day at school the master told me, before they were getting to go home, he wanted me to wait a few moments after the rest of the *childer*. I said I would and still I was kind of afraid that it was something I had done on my way going to school, or coming home, or maybe in the school. I didn't know but I was in a kind of dread that it was something like that. Home time came and they all cleared off. I sat on in my seat; Master Burke came down to me and told me he says, 'I hear the people say that you have "Tom Kelly making the poteen and the cow getting to the barrel"?' So I was kind of surprised at the time, but when I got a little time to think over I said I surely had got it. He says, 'Me and Mrs Connolly want you to get over a verse or two of it for us.' So I seen the thing was easy enough and I started and sung them the song.

## Tom Kelly's Cow

There's a boy in our country he's proper but small,
It's wee Tommy Kelly as we do him call.
It's him brews the cordial that exceeds them all,
He can beat all the Doctors from this to Fingal.

If you were sick and was ready to die
One glass of Tom's poteen would raise your heart high.
You could heave it up higher and nearer your nose,
It's an Irishman's toast then wherever he goes.

When the cow took a notion this drink for to take
She pulled and she pulled till she pulled out her stake.
She got to the barrel and she drank her fill
'Oh be-jeepers,' says Tom, 'she's left none for the "still".'

Next morning she awoke with a sad broken horn
Cursing the day and the hour she was born
She cursed Tom and John, Mr Beattie likewise
And all the *still-tinkers* that's under the skies.

Oh the cow came to Tom and she whispered in his ear
'You won't tell John that I got on the beer
If you don't 'pon my honour with a heart and a half
I will bring you against Lammas a fine heifer calf.'

They went up and had a talk among themselves after it. They
took fits of laughing at it and they come back down and each of
them gave me half-crown apiece. I know I went home in good
form, five bob at that time was a big thing. They were laughing
hearty when I left the school. I was very young at that time, I
wasn't too old fashioned even either, and to the day I left school,
and he was a cross master! He used to slap a lot of childer, he
never asked me to hold out my hand for a slap, no matter what I
done. Me and him was very intimate and he used to get me to do
wee things for him. Me and another lad the name of Mulladoon
used to be joulting about in an ass and cart bringing things up and
down to Aghadrumsee for him.

Of course everyone had the song at that time you know. After
it was made I heard it from a woman. She'd be a first cousin I'd

17

say of Tom Kelly's, she was Ned Boyle's wife. There's sons of hers down round about Belfast at the present time. It was their mother I heard at it. I had my own opinion who made the song. There was a friend of Tom's, he was a very good man at composing the verse of a song. He was the name of Tom Smith of Derrinabacco. He lived out in a very isolated place now. It's between this and Lisnaskea but it's far out from the road do you know. I wouldn't say for sure whether it was him composed this song or not, because I would think that this woman that I heard singing it she would be a good help to compose the song too, because she was a very good singer.

It was a very true story. I remember the time myself. I heard them talking about it. I would be seven or eight years old at that time. You see Tom, when he was making this drink, sometimes he'd go away into some public house and he might be drinking for a couple of days. The cows would have got no drink. He had maybe two or three or maybe four cows, I don't know what he had, and this barrel of stuff, you see, was set behind the cows in the byre. I suppose this cow she was getting no water and when she got dry enough she pulled her stake and got to the barrel and she drained it.

It was sung all round about here maybe when Tom would be there – it and 'The game-cock' and everything; that was another one was made on him sure. That was the same man you know – Tom wouldn't care.

There was a lot of boys from about our side at school you know, friends of mine that I was along with. When we got out at twelve o'clock of course our play was football, and sometimes Master Burke used to be out with us too. He was very fond of football. Some of them that would take a hatred against him, that he had slapped maybe before it, they'd try to give him a good kicking. Some of the childer wouldn't ask for better than that. They used to wear all clogs at them times you know, shoeings on them and shods. They used to peel his shins. Several times you'd see him taking up his trousers and looking at the blood running down his leg. But still and withal, even if he was short in the school he wasn't bad then, he'd only laugh at that now. He wouldn't say anything to them for hitting him a kick, he was good that way, the best!

On our way home, I suppose we were like all other childer, we'd be into orchards. They used *to view* us out of orchards that there was pears and apples in, and coming home from school we'd like a few of them. There was an old fellow used to view us constant. He'd take out the gun sometimes and fire a shot after us to scare us, right over our head you know.

But when we got home we were fairly tired you know. It was a fair walk and we might lie down and sleep. Maybe in an hour we'd be up again. We might meet some of our comrades in the evening and have another game of football. There used to be another game – skittles. Putting four there and one in the centre and three sticks to throw at them. We'd be at that at a crossroads too. They were made of ordinary wood cut out of the hedge and stood down usually always at a crossroads. Well you'd stand about ten to fifteen yards from them and you took three longer sticks and fired them to see what of them you could toss. The middle one was ten and the other four round was five. You competed against other you see. There might be a few on my side and a few on the other man's side and then whoever would have the most would be the winner. There used to be ha'pennies and pennies then bet on that you see. When you got up you played them too, I'd say up to twenty and twenty-five years of age, if you were good at them you see. Them that wouldn't maybe be playing skittles would bet pennies on you. There would always be one man to hold the bet and give it to the winner.

Of a Sunday evening there used to be football, *Gaelic football*. We would be having games of our own as younger ones do you know, not just into the line of the seniors. Well I remember specially one Sunday, it would be in the 'twenties, there was a team from Knockatallon and another team from Aghadrumsee. It was the final of the games that they had. So they differed about a point, that it should have been for Knockatallon. Two men got into a battle over the head of it, they struck with their fists. Then, of course, friends took in on both sides and it wasn't too long until the footballers and spectators and all was into a row. It lasted for maybe as good as fifteen or twenty minutes hard fighting. There was some got legs broken, some got arms broken. There was a lot of blood spilled about the field for a good while. But it was got settled up at the latter and they went home. It was nearly the last of the football on that field for a while, two or three years and maybe more. There's no football on it now but it's still known as the football field.

There was a few of them got into what they called the Red
Hands in Clones. They were a very good team at that time. They
were the name of Brian McMahon and his brother Patrick, and
there was another man from Knockatallon the name of Peter
McGeogh, he was very good too, a very strong man. Them men
got on very well at football. Brian McMahon's still alive yet but
he's not fit to be out. He's far over eighty years of age at this
present time.

Well just after this row was on the field it caused me not to be
very interested in football. I didn't like to see the row going on
or see anyone hurt so I hadn't a great interest in it afterwards.
There was an odd few got bicycles at that time. There wasn't very
many, people was all walking at that time nearly. But a few got
them and they were all new fangled with them at the time, and
they'd go long journeys. Of a Sunday evening there, if it was a
good evening, they might ride over forty or fifty mile maybe more.
Well I bought this bike off a young fellow at that time that set up,
he has a garage at the present time and he's going on very well,
the name of Sonny Elliot. I bought it for five guineas. It was a
Raleigh. They were the most popular in them days. Of course
there was Rovers and Cambridges and several other names of
bikes, but them was supposed to be the best stuff.

I remember me and a young fellow the name of Jimmy McCabe,
he's dead now Lord have mercy on him), we thought we'd take
out for a tour one day. So we travelled on and went away up
through *The Free State* and went on into Ballybay, Cootehill and
on up as far as Kill. There was a wee village there and we went in
to have some mineral or drinks, as we were dry of a warm evening
and what happened to be, but there was a wedding. There was a
fellow came out to the counter for to get a drink for the wedding
party that was in the room. He was from a place they called New-
bliss and he knowed me well. He had heard me singing some
place down the country, Newtownbutler or somewhere down
there, and he asked me to come in to sing a song. Well I wasn't
willing to go into a wedding party of course, but this young
McCabe fellow says 'Och! why wouldn't you? Sure we'll have a
good evening and never mind.' I went in and we had a great
evening in it. So we stayed that long that the boss of the place
put our bicycles on the back of the car. We'd too far a journey to
go and it was coming on to night and he left us at home and he

asked us to come up again. On different occasions he wrote to me to come up. Och! I never got up to it again.

There was no part hardly of Monaghan, Cavan, Fermanagh or Tyrone, but we done a bit of all anyway, maybe the most of it. But on this occasion we were down by the loughside, Lough Erne, and there was a society the time they called the Molly Maguires, they had a big meeting. We happened to run into them. We stayed the whole evening with them and on our way coming home, it was late in the evening, and this comrade of mine, Jimmy McCabe, says it would be worth the making a song on. And he says you were right good at poetry when you were at school and you might be fit to make one on it. So I made a bit of a . . . a few verses on it:

## The Molly Maguires

Oh it's in the praise of Molly's sons I'm going to sing a song;
They are a noble body, to her they do belong.
They are a noble body and they're sturdy stout and free;
They can root out all Defenders and plant the Laurel Tree.

'Twas on the seventeenth of March the weather was calm and
warm,
As I roved for recreation down by yon river Erne.
Where I espied a multitude of Molly's sons so gay,
And their music would delight you while the Ribbon Bands
did play.

I stood amazed, I on them gazed I wandered with surprise,
For the clothing that they wore it was dazzling to my eyes.
There was every lad, a handsome lass, with heart and hand
did go.
You would think that they came from Cornacreeve or Follom
down here below.

Now I will go down to Follom for to have an hour's spree,
Where the drums do neatly beat and their pipes do sweetly
play.
She says, 'Sure if I was a man along with you'se I'd gang,'
It's to maintain that conquerer's gain she's Molly that crossed
the line.

21

Now to conclude and finish I have no more to say,
May the Lord protect old Molly's sons at home and far away:
And when I'm on some foreign shore my fervent prayer will be
That the Lord may enable Molly's sons to tear down tyranny.

I made other songs but I wouldn't remember do you see, excepting that somebody reminded me. That 'Molly Maguires' I remembered that. There was someone asked me about it lately do you see and it just put me in mind of it. That's a political song. Sometimes the songs didn't suit several organizations, do you see, in the country. It could raise trouble in a house or a hall if you did sing a song. It could raise a wee disturbance even among our own population, catholic population. They didn't agree at that time at all, there would be plenty of battles between them. I seen it myself. I seen me singing a song away down at Cooneen, it ris trouble. There'd be a lot of people coinciding with one side of the party and the others wouldn't like it do you see. I suppose its much the same yet.

There was another chum of mine, he was the name of Paddy McCabe.* We got up to a lot of sport together. We used to always meet at this crossroads you know. There was a man took very ill and the Doctor came out. At them times there was very few cars. He had one of them and he left it at the crossroads. We were hanging about of course and we were anxious to know all about the car. We didn't see them at that time too often, excepting a car on the roads maybe once in six months. But me and Paddy got in and sat down in the car and I had been at the steering you see. Whatever way I managed to let off the brake, away she went and it was down an incline. It was fairly steep and on she went. I got her steered rightly for a time and I was going down to a bridge – it would be I suppose twenty-five or thirty perch down. I thought to myself I'd strike the ditch and I curbed her in and into the water-channel and she brushed up against the ditch just and stopped. Well we were annoyed because we thought we'd get jail for moving the Doctor's car. So we took in the fields that we wouldn't be caught on the road. We lent up and viewed to see the Doctor coming down again, we hid behind whin bushes – you often seen whins then, growing in the hedges – and stayed behind that for a while. We saw the Doctor coming down the

* No relation of Jimmy McCabe mentioned earlier in the chapter.

lane and he looked all round him. He looked down and turned and went away up the lane again, I suppose to look for help. So two or three of them come with him. They got her shifted out, she was only jammed up against the ditch in the water-channel, she was all right. 'Well do you know,' says Paddy, 'If this is known we'll get jail or be destroyed.' Says I, 'They could very ready take a couple of hundred pounds off us.' McCabe laughed at that. Taking a couple of hundred at that time! They never found out who did it. They may have thought that the car moved on herself now from the situation she was sitting in you know, maybe that he had forgot to put on the brake or something.

At that time I remember I used to take a great interest in *hunting*. When I used to see them out, coming on after the harvest-time when it'd be gathered, I took interest for a few years in hunting, and got a dog, a hound. It was called Comber. So I followed the hunting for a short time. On the 26th July there used to be a hunt on Clogher, that was in the summer-time. They never hunted about our side until all the crop was gathered, the corn and spuds and everything, they hunted till the winter-time. But at the 26th July they always had this hunt and many's the time I was on Clogher Mountain hunting.

We'd walk to it and back across the mountain to a place called the Red Barns, a big house up on the mountain and it was painted red. They hunted from that way down to near Clogher Valley. There was a lot of hares on that mountain you see, and they had a very good view of them. Although it was all heather there was nothing to prevent them seeing the hunting for a very long journey, they could see for miles around. So it was good sport now.

There's a great few hunting songs but I don't have them. There's one, I only heard a snatch of it. This old fellow sung it in Clogher as we were down for a drink one night. I was in the bar and he was in a room but I never seen him after it. He was an aged man at the time but he was a good singer. I didn't even know his name nor who he was, but he come from that locality, down about Clogher Valley there some place. He only sung a couple or three verses, but he apparently had it all, only he had some drink on him and people was continually asking him to sing more, but he didn't sing any more of it. I heard him singing this now:

## Hunting Song

There's another fine dog they call Timer,
He's yet the best hound ever run,
For when that the hare sees him coming,
She knows that her life's nearly run.

There is another fine dog they call Gay-Lad
When he thinks that they're quitting too soon
He will go by himself on the mountain
And will hunt by the light of the moon.

That was just what I heard of it do you know.

Another thing they usually always had in my early days was
cockfights and they have them yet. They all gather to some certain
place. Of course there would be nobody only the people that'd
have a game-cock for battles and some other team that'd be
against them. They had so many cocks to fight, six or seven on
each side, and they took on a battle and they bet some money on
it. They'd be at it in isolated places yet, all over the country.
There's been several battles lately in these late years.

You see these old men, or men that's used to the job, they'd
put what they call spurs on them. They're wee bits of steel, with
wee leather straps round the back of their leg. They're as sharp
as a needle. They put them on and leaves them down on *the pit*.
There's what they call two handers, they leave the birds down on
the pit and they go for other. Aye they put them down and let
them pick others heads, they dab at other first for a couple of
minutes maybe, and then they let them at it. Oh! several times
one kills other and sometimes they put eyes out of other, with
these steel spurs. Ach! it's a cruel business you know. I seen one
time, the blood was coming apparently out of the side of his head
or you'd think about the cock's ear, and this man sucked the
blood and sticked up this place that was affected whatever way
I didn't just see what he done. It healed up a kind of way and he
sucked the blood out with his mouth and put it into the game-
cock's beak again. Apparently it revived it.

There's a song about the battles. There was on one occasion
that they come down to Lurgan, that was a man the name of
Kelly, and they had battles against a party was down about

24

Portadown or Lurgan. I remember it all right but I was young at
that time for to go, but they made a song on it afterwards. I used
to hear an old fellow singing it in our country. He was very good
at it and I got him to sing it a couple of times for me so I picked
it up. He was a near friend of Tom Kelly's. He was the name of
Neill, Larry Neill. In fact he was down at these battles and helped
Tom for bring the birds down. They brought it in *raygo bags* at
that time, a stick rolled in the top of them. They'd get on the train
and go ahead with them. That's the way they carried them a lot
of times, excepting if it was a short journey they just carried them
in their hands.

Would you like to hear that song about it? I'll get over a bit of
it for you anyway:

## The Follom Brown-Red

Oh it's of a noted brown-red cock in Follom he did walk;
He learned his bold exercise, by Kelly he was taught.
They brought him down to Lurgan on the twelfth day of July,
For to fight against *a piley* cock the cheers would reach the sky.

Oh then up comes John O'Raven and he stepped intil the ring.
Saying, 'I'll make a pit for Kelly's cock let him either lose or
    win.'
There was some now for to laugh at him and some on him
    'til frown,
Saying, 'He'll never want a pit again if he pits Portadown.'

At the fourth now hard engagement the piley lost an eye
'Oh come on brown-red,' brave Larry said, 'you ne'er come
    here to die.'

Oh Larry to the station flew with a brown bird in his hand
He says to Josy Lutham, 'come hand him if you can.
Right well I know you are afraid your piley to lay down,
For he ne'er could fight that wee brown-red that was reared
    near Follom town.'

Here's a health to Tommy Kelly, long live his flock to reign,
And not forgetting Bob Maguire that assisted in the game.
Not like that traitor Purdy that all the world does know,
For he gained dishonour for us all, above all the roads he goes.

25

You see when these two birds met they let them pick other's heads first and they dropped on the ground then, after a few minutes, and they got into a fight. Well when they got into a fight, like men fighting or anything else, they got exhausted out till they got a wee bit of a rest. Their energy was all gone so they staggered about for a while and the men would lift them off the ground and hold them in their hand and rub their neck and sleek them down and *lay them ready* for another battle, that was another engagement. So they were put down again and that'd be the second fight till they'd get too wearied out and lose all their energy. They were lifted again on till the fourth engagement, you see, the brown-red struck the pilot in the eye and put an eye out of him. So it left him not too able to fight for a while. So they were afraid of the police coming to *the quarter* as they might come out of Lurgan, it wasn't so far out of it, and they were going to move to another place. So this man, he was a friend of Kelly's, the name of Neill, he lifted the bird in his hand and went along with this man that had the pilot from Portadown, and the two was walking along to another *station* where they would fight the battle out do you see. It might be other cocks would fight, it might be them two again. So he asked him, he says if you can *hand him?* So I don't know if they had another battle with them two or not. Purdy was another party that carried the game-cock traditional on and he took a spite at Kelly because they had some *differ* at cockfights before it; and they blamed him always for sending the police to Kelly's battles when they'd be any road, if he knowed about it. So then they called him a traitor.

# If you want your praties sprayed . . .

It wasn't all football after school of course. It's according to the time of year it'd be. If it was the time that the potatoes was digging you'd be out gathering potatoes after somebody that'd be throwing them out with a spade on the ridge. And if it was earlier in the season you helped to work at the corn, to tie corn and stook. And you wrought earlier again any time you could get to it at the hay, we'll say in the month of July. They never cut it sooner than the month of July or August at that time, and you wrought at the hay, that's what put in your time.

My father put in potatoes and corn. It was all done with a spade at that time. He kept some cattles, the cows for milk and he reared some of the calves on for *springers* and some of them was sold when they were eighteen months or two years old. They would put in onions and cabbages but just for themselves. There was no such a thing as a plough in them days. They harrowed the corn with a horse and harrow all right but, with the exception of putting out manure for the purty's, they done the rest with the spade. It's just the ordinary spade with the two lugs on it. In my early days that's all was wrought with, there was no ploughs. A McMahon spade was in our district at that time. McMahon made spades for all over Ireland you know, and parts of England and Scotland and everyroad else, but they all had a different type of a spade. There was some of them they called a three-quarter spade and there was some of them they called a full spade. The full spade would be a spade that a man would be digging lea ground with, that's where the green grass grows and where it never might be laboured before. That would be for the full spade he'd be digging that. There'd want to be a lot of steel and iron in that spade because many's a man in my early days wore two of them in the one season. He'd dig maybe two or three acres himself of lea ground for corn or potatoes or anything. The three-quarter spade was a lighter spade and longer. There was longer iron in it than the full spade but still it wasn't as strong nor it wouldn't stand as much abuse. There was what they called a turf spade too, there had to be a wing on the one side of it, the same as the part straight down. They use the spade a little in this part of the country yet now, you set a lot of potatoes. I have potatoes set out there in the corner. I set them with a spade and shovelled them with a spade, just the same spade.

McMahon's had two founderies – one up at Shannach there, it's just up there about a mile and a half towards Clones direction on that road up there, and at Lackey Bridge. He was Jemmy McMahon and that man's son, old John Pat McMahon, he has retired too. He stopped the job altogether. There's nobody making spades there now. It's only shortly you know they have retired you know. It's not two years yet since they quit them and they were making them in the same way, and shovels you see too. Them both mills are there all the time, but they're not used now. The mill was run by water. It was a big wheel that the water came down on and the water turned the wheel round all the time. Well then there was a big hammer that the water, when it fell on that, it lifted this big hammer. They called it the big hammer and it plated out the iron for the spade. There was a man there for plating them out first. There was another man coming for finishing them. There was another man coming to put the shaft in them. There was another man coming to put the head on them, the place that you catched your hand on the head of the spade. And there was all them was working one down from the other, from the man that was finishing them and the man that was shafting them, the man that was putting the heads on them. They were shafted with foreign wood. I think *the weight of* that was foreign wood, it was light wood you know, the shaft of the spade was light d'you know. In my early days sometimes we always cut *a sally* shaft out of the hedge and brought it to the mill and they put in that shaft and put a head on it for us, their own head, and that spade would only cost a half-a-crown. A new McMahon spade, I think it cost at that time about four shillings, or maybe three and nine-pence or something.

My mother she wrought in the house, she milked the cows and

fed the calves and pigs and everything like that. Just as every woman did at them times. There wouldn't be many sows, it wasn't like now. Maybe one or two sows kept about a house. She looked after them. She mostly always wore skirts and red petticoats. All colours of skirts you know, just like now. The women wore what they called cloaks and bonnets. They wore that to fair and market and to church and *chapel*. They would be dark, usually dark. The men nearly always wore these long what they called a clawhammer coat. You know swallow-tail or clawhammer they called it at them times. The trousers was fairly tight in them days too. After it they got a wee bit wider. Well this was dressing-up dress, I mean to say that was clothes you used to wear to market, I mean the men wouldn't work in that. Usually they wrought in sleeved waistcoats. They were a kind of *chammy* or leather kind of thing. They were made out of leather and some of them was made out of skin and they had sleeves in them but no collar.

Well when I was a young boy there was no potato only a Champion potato. There might be sometimes an odd Flounder, a very early potato. The Champion was a very good potato and was very dry, the best table potato was ever known, but after years it started to fail and failed on till they changed till another crop of purtys. That was Kerr's Pink and Aran Victor. I had that when I started on my own farm till I retired I might say.

You know they used to spray these potatoes, when I was a boy, with an ordinary heather besom tied with a string round it. They made the blue stone and lime, they used at that time with the blue stone, and they dipped it in the bucket and shook it on the potatoes. That's the way they sprayed them. But eventually it come on that they got what they called a spraying machine that you carried on your back. There was an old fella in our country, he was an old R I C man. He was on the police for many's the year, he got to be a sergeant. He told me himself that he served his time in a place they call Ballisadare in the County Sligo, and he was the first to get a spraying machine in the country. Nobody had a spraying machine and of course, they all called on the 'Sergeant' for to spray their purty's for them. He went round spraying four or five forty-gallon barrels in the day, round every neighbour in the country.

There was an old character in our country made a song on it. His name was William Quigley. He made a song on Sergeant

O'Neill and how he sprayed for everyman and how careful he was
at it. The song of it wasn't too long now. I'll give you all I know of
it anyway:

## Sergeant Neill

If you want your praties sprayed, well you can call on Sergeant
    Neill.
Oh he's the boy that'll do it well, and he'll not destroy your
    kale.
He sprayed for lame James Blakely, and he sprayed for
    George's Bill,
And he sprayed for 'Long John' Gawley, that lives upon the
    hill.

He sprayed for Peter Lowry and he sprayed for Larry's Hugh,
And he turned to Greaghollia and he sprayed for Bishop
    Grew.
He sprayed for Patrick Anthony and for the Widow's Pat
And he sprayed for John the Carpenter, that wore the
    three-cocked hat.

He sprayed for the McGrory's, that lived up at the Road,
And he sprayed for Paddy Berry, that lives in Mullin's Cove,
He sprayed for Tommy Armstrong, that kept the kicking
    mule;
And he sprayed for decent Robert Ellett, that hopped round
    upon the stool.

That's the song he made on it.
    The reason why I think they had nicknames was that there was
too many of the one name in that district, do you know? We'll
say there was too many Maguires, there was too many O'Neills.
They had to put some separate name on them to know them.
That was the reason they called them nicknames. They called me
'John Jock' and me father before me got that name, because there
was too many Maguires in the place. It still carries on.
    Anyway when I was a boy, before I left home, it was a very bad
season. It was wet and the Champion purty's all failed. Before the
people got time to spray them they had been killed with blight,
and I remember digging with a brother of mine a whole day, with

two spades, for potatoes. I carried them down to the house, about
four or five stone, after working hard the whole day, two of us.
They weren't bigger than generally *marls*.

Well that bid to be around the 'twenties or before it that them
potatoes failed. They were very bad times for farmers, very bad.
They had no potatoes and potatoes was their main crop, and corn
at that time. The corn didn't fail, but the potatoes was their main
feeding crop rather than hay. They depended actually on them
the whole season round. They had a lot of them in. They might
have thirty or forty ton of purty's do you see, and it kept the
animals going, and themselves. I remember in the later days,
when the Champions had all run out nearly round our part of the
country, being in Lisnaskea in with the Chemist man and we were
talking about potatoes. 'Well, that's a very strange thing,' said I,
'I thought them had died out altogether.' So he says, 'I'm getting
*a hundred* every week from a man out here, a couple of mile out
the road.' Well he said they were marvellous for eating. So I
asked him if I could have any and he says, 'the next time he comes
in I'll get you a few stone.' I think he got me a couple, maybe
four stone of them. So I have them planted at the present time
and they're the best eating spud yet, of any of them. No matter
what kind you get there's nothing like the Champion potato.

When it would come to harvest-time there'd be always a lot of
help would come into the field. Even young boys that would be
at school with you would come in to help if you were at a field of
meadow hay. Neighbours helped each other. You helped me and
I helped you, that's the way they wrought in them days. They
don't do it as much now but if you had your corn cut and some
other neighbour beside you hadn't, you went to him and helped
him to he cut he's and he comes to you and helped you to put in
your corn, and so on that way. Sometimes a man might be lying
in hospital, he might be sick or the man might have died and the
wife had no help other than her neighbours to do. Their corn
would be lying there to cut, so the neighbours all around about
would go to that man and bring their weapons with them, hooks and
scythes, and cut his harvest and it was said that that was *a mechal* at
that house. That's what it was called.

The hay was cut with a scythe, and the corn a good deal of it
was cut with a hook with teeth in it. You shored it and made a
strap for the sheaf. About three handfuls made a good sheaf you

31

see. Then you put it up in stooks. You put it up we'll say about twelve along and two on the sides and the four hoods on and it kept there till you put it in the stack. You know they'd start to shear corn and at that time it was all in ridges, every man had his own ridge to shear. Well I often seen them in a rush to see who'd get to the head first. There was some old men was great now, they could go up it as quick as a machine, nearly, shearing. Well when these men would all be shearing with hook you see and when they'd come to have the field nearly finished they might leave fifteen or twenty stalks of corn growing up in the corner. So they'd all take and see which of them could cut them stalks down by throwing the hook at them. So there was some of them very good at it that might be fit to cut all the stalks down, and some of them might take three or four of them, or five maybe. There used to be the usual thing whoever cut the last of them here they took it home with them. Whatever they done with it I couldn't know, they had some idea of their own of it.

There was a song about the barley grain, they had it in them times. I have none of it you know, but here's what I have:

## John Barleygrain

Oh John Barley is the rarest grain,
That e'er you sowed on land.
It far exceeds than any other grain
With the cast that you give your hand.
Ah to the legum ba tarry oodle ah
John Barleygrain's for me.

Lord have mercy on my father he had that way of it.

In my early days people that hadn't work at home, that hadn't a big farm or something to work at, they hired with some other gentleman for six months. In every small town in the country there was a hiring fair – they had a certain day for it. There'd be an ordinary fair day and a hiring day and there was some places that had a hiring fair just on its own. They had that in the town of Clones. The hiring fair was always held in May, it would be the first or second Thursday in May in Clones, and the same in November when their six months would be up. It could happen on a fair day, or it could happen on a middle-market day, but it was Thursday always. It's well back now, over thirty-five years since I remember a hiring fair. It was the day for everyone changing places that were working. A man working for the last six months, we'll say with some man, he would be changing or maybe staying on. If he was staying on there'd be no call for him going to the hiring fair. The man would give him maybe the same wages, or maybe more, to stay for another six months with him. But the men or women that was leaving the place that they wrought for the last six months, they went to this hiring fair and hired with some different man. They'd think maybe they weren't getting enough money, or they mightn't be well treated about the place and they'd change. They might get a pound or two more and if they were well treated they stayed with him for years.

Everyone in the country would know of course who was working-men and working-women. If they didn't know they'd inquire off their neighbour did he know of anyone that would hire for six months. Well that neighbour would bring them to that man and they'd have a bargain. They'd go into a public house and they'd have a couple of drinks and they'd have a bargain at how much he was going to be hired. He hired him there and then at whatever. There was a lot of variations in the wages you know at that time. It would be a big thing at that time, a few pound. There could be a few pound of a variant take place. Some had six pounds for the six months only, and others had seven and eight and nine pound. It was according to the place they were working and who they were working with. Some would have more to do than others, a lot more stock about the place and a lot more farming to be done, more crop and potatoes and corn and everything else. He would ask the man what did he expect for the six months and of course he would try to take him as low as he could. Then he would give him a little track of money, a few shillings. He was hired then when he got those few shillings, maybe five bob or ten bob. They had some special name for it, I don't remember it now. It got *earnest*, it was something like that.

At that certain set time of the year there'd be a lot of *trick o' the loops* and *wheels of fortune* men about the Diamond in Clones. There might be an odd one at other times but *there inclined to be* far more of these about at the hiring fairs, because the crowds would be bigger you know. What would be out for hiring at that time would be a very big party of people. There'd be thousands out. There wasn't that many farmers and the country was thickly populated. You see the families was very big, there might be three and four and five out of one house would be hiring.

They'd be mostly single boys and girls would be hiring at that time. If a man got married he done the same what he does now. He took up house and he wrought away and hired on. The girl might work for a while with the same man, or she might be working for a different man. There's a song, I believe it was my mother that I heard at it, and of course Biddy and Brian sings it too.

## The Strabane Hiring Fair

From Omagh town unto Strabane one morning as I took my
    way,
Sure all along the road seemed thronged with lads and lasses
    fine and gay.

It was there I spied a charming wee maid, she was walking
    slowly by herself,
For a-fear the rain her clothes would stain I did extend my
    umberel.

'How far do you travel along the road on this fine summer's
    morning oh!'
'It's 'til Strabane,' she kindly says, 'do you not know this is
    hiring day?'

'I fear the day it will be wet, although the morning does look
    fine
I fear my love,' she then did say, 'we won't be in for hiring
    time.'

'Well if you consent to have a glass, let it be brandy, ale or
    wine,
We'll take a glass and then we'll pass and reach Strabane for
    hiring time.'

She gave consent, away we went unto an ale-house by the way;
Glass after glass the time did pass, to we both forgot it was
    hiring day.

The clock struck three she smiled at me, 'Kind servant boy
    the fault is thine,

34

The evening's wet and we're far from home, forby we missed
  our hiring time.'

'Cheer up, cheer up my bonny wee lass, I do not mean to
  harm you.
For a marriage now I mean to try, for a servant boy proves
  always true.'

'To marry a man I am too young, besides my mother has
  none but me
But I'll comply and I'll never deny I'll marry before I hire
  again.'

That night we spent in merriment and married we were next
  day;
And every now and then she'd smile, and my hiring time was
  knocked astray

Let lads and lasses all be true and listen to these couple of
  lines;
If you take a glass too long to last, you're sure to miss your
  hiring time.

I remember a big hiring fair in Rosslea. Of course of the 8th of
May it was always very big, and I remember a big man, his name
was 'Big Phil'. He had a terrible loud voice and he stood about
seven foot. I think he only wanted about an inch off seven foot.
He was over twenty stone weight and he was fond of *a half-one*
like manys another man and when he got one he'd talk very loud.
There was only a couple or three police, two constables and a
sergeant in Rosslea at the time. But this was a new recruit that
come from Enniskillen and the Sergeant sent him down for to
make Phil be quiet, that he was talking too loud or he'd take him
up to the barracks. Of course he knowed the kind of Phil all right
for the Sergeant had seen him before. So he went up to Phil this
young recruit and he says, 'If you don't be quiet I'll have to take
you up to the barracks.'
  Well Phil looked down at him, 'Holy Moses,' he says, 'You'll
take me to the barracks?'
  'Aye.'
  'Who sent you to do that?'

'The Sergeant,' he says, 'sent me down to make you be quiet or I'd have to take you up to it.'

'Well I wishst,' he says, 'the Sergeant was down here.'

So he threw his arm round the policeman, in under his arms and stepped away up an entry with him, and the policeman's heels was kicking like a gypsy woman with a child. Ah! he played it for to get loose and he'd go back to the barracks. 'Oh no,' Phil says, 'you'll never see the barracks again child, I'll drown you in this pond at the back of the village.' So there was a few neighbours that knew Phil all right and went up after him and interceded with Phil to let him go and Phil shouted after him, 'If I ever see you again about the town, I'll make a parable of you.'

They had the ordinary fair in Clones every month and then there was what they called the middle-market every fortnight. This always happened on a Thursday – the fair-day and the middle-markets. There wasn't any cattle brought out to the middle-market. There was pigs and small calves, what they called *drop-calves* sold on the Diamond, and potatoes and oats and hay and everything else was sold on it, in the middle-market. But there was no large cattle or springers.

Of course things is changed a whole lot now. The creamery was started we'll say in 1920 or '21 or '2, in our locality anyway. And when the milk started to flow to the creameries they were no longer churning in a churn at home or putting butter in tubs for sale in the markets. They're selling the milk to the creamery in creamery cans now you see.

Then they put up these marts. They are not long in our district only ten or fifteen years. The auctioneer sits there and the cattle's turned into the ring and the highest and best bidder gets. It has all changed. The fairs was all done away with, and markets, and there's none in our locality now at all. But they say that up in the Republic of Ireland they have an odd fair yet. They bring horses to it and calves and cows but there's none down round our side. There's a lot of people *doesn't care about it*, they'd rather have to open fair and market. It wasn't as costly. You see that auctioneer has to be paid. There was no auctioneer when they were selling on the public green, as they called it. You had no fees for to pay when the beast was sold. The buyer and the seller made their own bargain and it was a lot cheaper. I remember a long time ago I went to Clones with my father in a pony and cart, and at that time

36

when they had their marketing done there was always ballad singers on the Diamond. They sung lots of songs and they told you before it what the song was. And there was a wee boy would go about with a great lot of them in his hand and he would sell to the people round about. They were priced from about twopence to threepence apiece and I remember they used to get them all sold every one of them. Nearly everyone bought *a ballad*.

I remember one especially that this ballad was bought off them. He was more interesting than the rest of them because he wore a fairly long beard and he had a wee girl with him who played an ordinary fiddle, and she was very good too! Sometimes he would be out and dance a step to her playing, as well as singing a song. He sold the most ballads I think of the lot now. He was singing this song about people sailing away to America and my father bought the ballad. So I got it in my pocket and was very fond of it and kept it. I have the song yet.

## Thousands Are Sailing to America

Oh you brave Irish people, wherever you be,
I pray stand a moment and listen to me.
Your sons and brave daughters are now going away,
And thousands are sailing to America.

CHORUS

Ah good luck to them now, and safe may they land,
They are pushing their way to a far distant strand,
For here in old Ireland no longer can stay,
For thousands are sailing to America.

Oh the night before leaving they're bidding goodbye;
And it's early next morning their hearts give a sigh.
They will kiss their dear mothers and then they will say,
Goodbye father dear I'm now going away.

CHORUS

Oh their friends and relations and neighbours also
They're packing their trunks now ready to go,
When the tears from their eyes it run down like the rain,
And the horses were prancing going off for the train.

CHORUS

It is now you will hear that very last cry,
And a handkerchief waving and bidding goodbye.
The old men tells them be sure 'til write
And watches the train till she goes out of sight.

CHORUS

It is God help the mother that rears up a child,
It is now for the father he labours and toils.
He tries to support them he works night and day
And when they are reared sure they will go away.

CHORUS

The ballad singers were especially around 1908 or '10, to 1916 to '17. That was the time I mostly seen them. When I was home out of Scotland on a holiday, that'd be between '24 and '25, I'd say, I inquired was there any ballad singers and they said there didn't come a ballad singer to Clones for twelve or eighteen months before that. They said they had disappeared.

There was plenty of other ballads. When Fee killed Flannigan there was ballads printed on it all right. But I heard a man, he was a kind of poet, beside myself, he made a song. It was a wee bit different, not too much from the ballad, but it was much longer. Many's the time he sung the song for me. He was the name of William Quigley. It was a very lonesome thing to happen. It happened in Clones about 1912 – it might be about 1910 or sooner. I just heard them talking about it and singing the song you know. They said it was a very outrageous doing and a very cold-blooded murder, the way it happened. They were two comrade boys you see, it was bad for to see it happening between the two. This was the song this old gentleman made on it.

## Fee and Flannigan

Oh you feeling hearted Christians wherever you may be,
I'll call on God for mercy, I hope you pray for me.
It's true that I'm found guilty, and (in) shame I now must die,
I'm lodged in Armagh County Jail, my sentence for to try.

'Twas on the sixth of April I mind that awful day,
When young Joe Fee the prisoner, he brought young John
    away.
He brought him from his work about one o'clock that day,
Ah he killed him in a slaughter house on Clones market day.

'Twas for the greed of money he killed his comrade boy,
Oh such a wilful murder was done in Clones town,
And buried him in a dung yard, thinking he'd ne'er be found.

But when he had him buried he thought all things was right;
It was in nine months after when the murder came to light;
The police were alarumed and Fee they did surround,
They took him on suspicion and handcuffed he was bound.

Oh handcuffed he was bound brave boys, to Armagh was sent
    down,
He was there till the July assizes, all waiting for his crime.

It being on the eighth November, it'll be remembered well,
When Fee's mother and sister went to take the last farewell,
It would grieve the heart that sight to see, and vain they did
    deplore,
For to see them meet in a dark, dark cell, and part for
    evermore.

Oh the Jury found him guilty and the judge made this reply,
'On the twenty-second September you are condemned to die.'

On the twentieth September it was in the following year,
The priest he put on his robes and thus to him did say,
You come now Joseph Fee for your time is near an end.
You come and take this crucifix, with spirits follow me
Oh you have to meet your merciful God that died on Calvary.

'Twas early the next morning at the hour of eight o'clock,
When the murderer of John Flanagan stood at that fatal dock.
He bade adieu 'til all his friends before the world to be,
And in a minute after, he was in Eternity.

Saying fare ye well to Clones town where I spent many's the
    year and day,
Likewise unto that slaughterhouse from you I now must go
    away.

39

Good Christians all, both great and small I hope you pray
   for me.
The bolt was drew, and Fee soon flew on to Eternity.

I remember another song that that old poet as we called him
round our side used to sing, when me and him would be working
together. We wrought together. He was an old man but I was
only very young at the time.


## The Constant Farmer's Son

There was a rich farmer's daughter near Limerick town did
   dwell;
She was modest fair and handsome, her parents loved her well.
She was admired by lords and squires, but all their hopes in
   vain;
There was but one young farmer's son now Mary's heart did
   gain.

Long time young Willie courted her they appointed the
   wedding day.
Her parents give consent but her brothers they did say,
'There's one young lord has pledged his word and we will
   not him shun,
For we'll betray and surely slay your constant farmer's son.'

The fair being held near to that town her brothers went
   straightway,
They asked young William's company with them to spend the
   day.
The fair was gone and night came on and they swore that his
   race was run,
And with their sticks the life did take of her constant farmer's
   son.

Oh Mary on her pillow lay she had an awful dream,
She dreamt she saw her true love lying dead in yon purling
   stream.
Mary arose, put on her clothes, to seek her love she ran,
It was pale and cold she did behold her constant farmer's son.

She took him by the lily-white hand she kissed him o'er
  and o'er,
And to release her troubled mind she kissed him o'er again.
She pulled the green leaves off yon trees, to shade him from
  the sun.
Three nights and days she passed away with her constant
  farmer's son.

The hunger pain came creeping on and this poor girl wept
  with woe.
And for to find the murderers it's homeward she did go.
It's parents dear or did youse hear that dreadful deed that's
  done
In yonder vale lies cold and pale my constant farmer's son.

Down came the eldest brother and said, 'It was not me,'
And so replied the younger one and swore it bitterly.
Hold down your heads don't go so red, but try the law to shun
Youse have done the deed and youse'll bleed for my constant
  farmer's son.

These villains they were found guilty and for that same did
  die,
The doctors got their bodies all for to practice on,
In a madhouse cell young Mary dwells for her constant
  farmer's son.

I went home with that man one night and we met a little light
on the road coming along about a foot or a foot and a half off the
ground. It passed by and the man was a kind of daunted at the
time. Of course I thought it was some small light or some small
child that was carrying a lamp. It was more like a hurricane lamp.
He was a kind of afraid of it. I had many's the time to go home
with him when he'd be in our house after it, for fear he'd meet it.
We met it on two or three occasions after that. I never could tell
what it was but they used to call it 'Willy the Wisp'. I saw this
light they called Willy the Wisp myself and it was floating about
round the fields as quick as flash of lightning nearly. It isn't that
long ago since I did see it. This wasn't going very quick. It was
going very slowly along the road. I never could tell what it was.
I met it myself coming home too on the same road without this

old man. I haven't seen it recently; it's a long period of time, twenty years since I seen it. It's a mystery.

I was interested in his songs and I used to keep him singing back and forward. This is another song I learned:

## Young Mary from Kilmore

You gods of love I pray draw near and lend to me some aid;
It's here I am endeavouring to praise a charmin' maid.
She's proper, tall and handsome, has a-wounded my heart
    sore,
Oh she is the blooming fair one, young Mary from Kilmore.

This young man says, 'My charming maid I'll give to you my
    hand,
My father he has promised me all his houses and free land,
Beside you are the only one my parents do adore.
They say they would do all they could for the maid of sweet
    Kilmore.'

'Oh,' she says, 'young man let go me hand, and don't praise
    me so high,
For I'd think it far more pleasure for you to pass me by,
My parents of times told me with you to court no more,
And I think by them I'll be advised and stop in sweet
    Kilmore.'

For there is three heroes go this way, I heard the people say,
That is bold Gunn and McIlroy and Maguire from Rosslea.
But let them all say as they will, for me I'll say no more,
They need not think to banish me from the shades of sweet
    Kilmore.

Now to conclude and finish my pen I'll take in hand,
John O'Brien is my name and flowery is my land,
But since she has deceived me on her I'll write no more,
But she's still that blooming fair one, young Mary of Kilmore.

# Oh grass may grow and waters flow . . .

When I was round about twenty years of age and maybe twenty-one, I was going to a dance here and there to halls and country houses. Me and a comrade I had, the name of McCabe, he used to always travel along with me. We'd have girl-friends and we'd see them home no matter what time it was. The parents never minded, but at that time you know some of the clergy, it wasn't just about our place but near by, they would rather that they'd be separated altogether, the women go home themselves and the men go by themselves. They done that in a lot of places. Clergy visited places to see that they'd go home single. It wasn't in our area but it was near by.

Well every house in our part of the country near by was *a ceilidhing house* at that time. They just danced in the kitchen or maybe if they had a big barn outside. If there was many gathered in do you see they went out to the barn, where they kept corn and spuds and everything in the winter-time. They had a night in the week maybe for ceilidhing 'til some separate house. They'd go to that house and it just happened to be if there came in many ceilidhers to a house they'd strike up a wee bit of a dance. If there wasn't a music man there they sent for him.

They were visited once or twice a week according to the many houses that was knocking around. There would be maybe three or four ceilidhs or dances a week. If there come any visitors it might be every night in the week. There'd come visitors maybe from Dublin or Galway, or Leitrim or Limerick or some of them places to see friends. They called them tramps at that time. They'd say there was a tramp in such a house. They went every night to that house that week, maybe danced till daylight in the morning, had some *sprees*. I remember an old boy used to sing a song at the sprees, about sailing away 'til America. The start of it was 'Farewell dear Erin I now must leave you and cross the seas to a foreign clime. Farewell to friends and kind relations until my parents I left behind.' I'll sing it for you now:                    .

## My Charming Mary

Farewell dear Erin, I now must leave you
And cross the seas to a foreign clime.
Farewell to friends and kind relations,
and 'til my parents I left behind.

Farewell green hills, and your sweet lovely valleys,
Where with my love I did of times roam,
And fondly told her I ne'er would leave her,
While walking in yon silent grove.

But I must leave you my charming Mary,
Where we spent many's the happy day,
With lads and lasses and sporting glasses,
But now I'm bound for Americay.

Oh charming Willy you do not leave me,
I loved you dearly right well you know.
Pray do not stray to a foreign nation,
To leave us here love in grief and woe.

I know right well that the times they're changed love,
It causes thousands to go away,
But if you'll wait unto the next season,
We'll both sail off to Americay.

My dear have patience, my charming Mary,
You'll crown my labour, believe what I say.
I will return love with gold and store
And I'll take you off to Americay.

And when I'm rolling upon the ocean,
Sweet Mary dear you are in my mind.
So do not mourn love, for I'll return love,
If you prove constant, sure I'll prove kind.

So my dear have patience, my charming Mary,
And fare ye well love, I must away.

For I do intend it, let none prevent it,
To seek the adventures of Americay.

Unknown 'til parents friends and relations,
My dearest Willy with you I'll roam.
For I have plenty to take us over,
As you won't consent love to stay at home.

He gave consent then straightway they went it,
And soon got married without delay.
One hundred pounds then she did leave down,
Sayin' love we'll be crowned in Americay.

I remember nearly the first dance I enjoyed in my life. I would be about eighteen or nineteen at the time. I never enjoyed anything as much. We went to a house in Carnmore. That's in the New-townbutler–Cranny direction. They were the name of Hardin, he was a Tommy Hardin. He had two or three sisters and the mother was living at the time too.

The dance at that time was old Irish music of course, a fiddle or a tin whistle. If that wasn't handy there was *a trump* or a mouth-organ, what they called a french-fiddle, till the fiddle would come, and if there was none of them you lilted or whistled for them till they did come. And they danced on till two or three in the morning maybe. Irish reels and jigs and another called the set o' quadrilles, all of them kind of dances. When they'd be tired dancing they'd get somebody to sing a song or maybe somebody might make a recitation.

When the dance would be going on about a couple or three hours someone might say, 'ought we not have a wee bit of a spree'. Well there'd be a good lot like to see it, so they'd put round the cap and whatever you threw into it, a shilling or sixpence or two shillings or whatever you had they went for a jar of whiskey. It wasn't too dear at them times you know. I bought some whiskey myself, at a shilling a half-pint, good whiskey! They'd come home with it and they'd put it round and it was drinking. Most of the men was all taking a sup. It left the place jollier. The girls might get a cup of tea, but men didn't get any at that time at dances.

So there gathered a fair wee crowd, it was of a Sunday evening. At that time people wasn't interested in dressing up so well. You might have a pair of clogs on you or your old jacket, you weren't too exact. The young girl of the house, she was Bridget, she had *a melodium*. She played for them dancing and they said, coming on for nine o'clock, that we'd better have a wee bit of a spree. A spree they called it if they were sending for some wee drop of drink. So they collected up anyway. Put round the cap as usual and a pair of fellas went away and they come back with a jar of *the clear stuff*, the mountain dew as they called it. We had a great night's dancing and singing. There was a lot of old fellas could tell bits of stories at the time. I don't mind any of the stories now but I remember an old fella, Joe Higgins, used to sing a song. He sung it that night too. He was married for years and a good deal of the family was grown up, but he still ceilidhed about. It was an unusual thing for married men to ceilidh about, but an odd few of them did. Their wives passed no remarks on that you know, but times they wouldn't be too agreeable. I think I have that song he used to sing anyway.

## Joe Higgins

Oh my name is Joe Higgins, a farmer by nigh,
I courted a lass but she was very shy.
She asked me to the kitchen for a moment or two,
'Well I'm danged but', says Joe, 'I don't care if I do!'

Da-di-fan-da-do-a-in sing tan-din-an-ee.

She brought me upstairs then to make things all right,
And six pints of porter I shoved out of sight,
Oh she says, 'My dear Joe would you have another or two?'
'Well I'm danged but', says Joe, 'I don't care if I do?'

Da-di-fan-da-do-a-in sing tan-din-an-ee.

Oh I hugged her and squeezed her with fond love of life,
She says, 'My dear Joe you might make me your own little
    wife.'
Ah when Joe heard this he stuck to her like glue,
'Well I'm danged but', says Joe, 'I don't care if I do!'

Da-di-fan-da-do-a-in sing tan-din-an-ee.

It was early next morning they went to get wed,
The parson he opened the book and he said,

46

'Ah it's you'll take with Joe, aye and Joe'll take with you,'
'Well I'm danged but', says Joe, 'I don't care if I do!'

Da-di-fan-da-do-a-in sing tan-din-an-ee.

It's now we are married, we're happy to be,
There's little no wee 'uns to annoy Joe or me.
Ah she says, 'Perservere and there might be a few,'
'Well I'm danged but', says Joe, 'I don't care if I do!'

Da-di-fan-da-do-a-in sing tan-din-an-ee.

It's now we are married we're living content,
Two wee 'uns we have got, but not the third yet.
Ah she says, 'My dear Joe, I'd like another or two,'
'Well I'm danged but', says Joe, 'I don't care if I do!'

Da-di-fan-da-do-a-in sing tan-din-an-ee.

It's now I have sung and I hope I pleased all,
I won't sing again if it's on me you call,
I won't sing again or I'm danged if I do,
Da-di-fan-da-do-a-in sing tan-din-an-ee.

That was the song he sung that night. I thought it that good that
I went to him afterwards and got him to sing it for me till I'd pick
it up.

Aye I mind that night well. I happened before we left to fall in
love with the youngest of the house, Bridget, that played the
melodium and I acquainted that house for years, till they all left
and went to Ameriky. She corresponded, wrote to me back and
for'ard and was wanting me to go out there. Well I didn't incline
to go. She's living yet, the only one of them I think that is. I never
saw her again. She married and had a daughter I know.

I was in that house another night but there was a different
character of a man in it. He was an aged man, over seventy years
of age at the time. He was Michael Nann, great sport for reading
books and he was a kind of *rebel* at that time. He used to sing an
odd verse. I remember he used to sing one about O'Donohue
that was born in Dublin. He went over it a couple of times for
me and I took an interest in the song and an interest in him
talking. At that time I took more interest in him than I would in
a young boy d'you know. He talked about this Jack Donohue

47

man. He told me about the time of the old *Fenians* long ago. He
said they made songs on them at that time. When they were
deported out to other countries there was no change on them, they
still kept to be rebels out in them countries.

I'll sing his verse now for you:

## Bold Jack Donohue

Oh in Dublin town I was brought up, that city of great fame,
My parents reared me tenderly and many do know the same.
For being a bold United boy they sent me across that main,
For seven long years to New South Wales, to wearing a
      convict chain.

I was not long there landed, upon the Australian shore,
Till I turned out, brave Irish boys, as I'd oftimes done before.
There was McNamara in yonder woods and Captain McAtee,
They being the chief associates of Bold Jack Donohue.

Oh Donohue was taken, it was for a notorious crime,
His sentence was for to be hung upon the gallows high.
But when he went to Sydney jail he left them all in a stew,
For when they went to call the roll they missed Jack Donohue.

When O'Donohue made his escape to the woods he took his
      way,
No tyrant dare show their face 'twas e'er by night or day,
And every week in the newspaper there'd be something
      published new,
Concerning our brave Irish lad they call Jack O'Donohue.

As O'Donohue was walking one Sunday afternoon,
When little was his notion that death would come so soon.
When a Sergeant of the Horse Police there charged his carbine,
He loudly cries O'Donohue you'll fight or else resign.

Oh resign to you you cowardly dog it's a thing I ne'er will do,
For I'll range those woods and valleys like the wolf or the
      kangaroo.
Before I'll work for Government men cried famed Jack
      Donohue.

Oh nine rounds this horse policeman fired, when at length the
    fatal ball,
Lodged in the breast of O'Donohue that caused him for to
    fall;
And as he closed his mournful eyes to this world he bade
    adieu;
Good Christians all now both great and small pray for Jack
    Donohue.

Well I made a drop of poteen in my early days of course, for a
spree. I've made none for years now. They made it with sugar and
yeast. You *stepped* the sugar in boiling water, so many gallons to
the stone. You put a pound of yeast to every stone of sugar and
then put in currants and raisins, tied them in wee bags and
dropped them into it to soak for the flavour. Some put apples in
it, apples that'd be lying there for a period of time you know and
got very ripe. The very ripe apples it was left a good flavour on
the drink. You got about six and eight pints from a stone of sugar.
    Well you leave that there till it's finished *working*. It works like
ale-plant, till it be's working about ten days or a fortnight and
then it finally stops when it has all the sugar and everything else
cut off. Then it's ready for the still.* There's several kinds of
still they used, in old times there was a big pot that would hold
about twenty gallons. You'd have a whole lot of whiskey off that.
We'll say you had about eight stone of sugar, you'd have about
sixty or seventy pints off it, if it went on well. There would be a
head made for that, by what they called a cooper, of oak and it
well hooped like a barrel. It's made the fit for the pot in under
but it develops out then to be wider at the top. A hole was cut
in the upper side for the arm. That's the article that goes from that
head 'til the worm that would be put in a barrel of cold water. I
mind this equipment made for making poteen. He was a gypsy on
the roadside, they called them tinkers at that time, and he made
it out of copper. Of course this man got him the copper and he
made it for him, a still and a head and coiled the worm and all for
him. So he wouldn't be too long at the job altogether. About a
week he had it for him. So he come round with *the tackle* to this
man, indeed I seen this tackle myself. It was just as nice a way of
making drink as ever I seen anywhere. I think he charged him

* See Plate 2.

49

*thirty-five bob* for making it and he got him the copper. There was men about the country could make some of *the articles* themselves but they couldn't coil the worm right, they could make an arm or . . . The gypsies nearly always made them. So you put fire 'til that and it wouldn't be too long till you'd have *drink*. The steam rises off the pot of *wash* below. It develops up and goes out through that arm and into the worm and it finally comes down as *the first shot*. That's the first time you put it through. You could drink it but it would be a small quantity of it, but it would be very little. It was too strong. A half one of it, there would be more in it than a half pint of whiskey what you would be getting across the counter from a publican.

They usually always distilled it twice now. They had the first coming down of that what they called *singlings*. So when it was finished the head was took off, the wash was threw out. A pail of spring water or clear water of any kind was put in the bottom of the pot and you put in the singlings and you run it again the same as the first time. They called it doubled at that and that was drink.

I suppose they made it because the whiskey was too dear to buy and a lot of them made it for their own use. Then some of them made it for publicans which bought it off them and sold it across the counter. Sometimes they used lemonade or maybe they used tea for colouring it, a drop of black tea. Them that'd be selling it to the publican they'd get a good thing out of it in the week. I remember it'd be about eight shillings a pint – that was in the 'twenties then. It went so great a pitch of making it about our side. There was plenty of poteen made and the Bishop condemned it altogether. It was a mortal sin to make poteen. The young fellows, even to the young boys of twelve and fourteen years of age, they were drinking it and it set them mad altogether. I think that was the reason he condemned it. There was a lot of people caught round about here. Several in my time. But they'd be informed on you know by some people. Fathers and mothers that would have young fellows taking drink and they didn't want to see that carrying on, so they'd inform the police about it. And a lot of times the police didn't want to catch these men either, for many's the time they could take a sup of it themselves if they got it. That was the main reason why they were caught, young people getting drink and going mad over the head of it.

There would be some people that would have a spite at one

1 The family tea

2    The poteen-still in this photograph shows all the parts mentioned
by John in chapter 4. The worm, of course, is hidden in the
barrel of water on the left. In this the steam from the pot
condenses into poteen. Nowadays bottled gas is probably a
more popular firing agent than the turf used in this scene.
There is no smoke with gas and thus less danger of being
discovered. The photograph was taken by W. A. Green on the
Inishowen peninsula in Co. Donegal c. 1926

another and it could be done that way too. If they were caught
red-handed we'll say making the drink they got three months or
six months in jail. I know plenty of them got as far as six months,
fined as well maybe fifty pound. Well, of course, when the police
would come there they'd spill all the drink, the ale and poteen
whatever of it was run, and they'd take the articles all with them,
into a lorry or jeep and take them all with them. Many's the time
that happened.

There's a song I got from a neighbour called James Gallagher,
over fifty years ago. It's about a man – they called them 'the
Revenue' long ago – that used to be. He got information where
poteen was a-making. He was going about, a local man maybe.
You might know him well enough but you mightn't know his job.
He could get the information of where it would be made and bring
the Revenue or police on you. There was none in my time, they
went a long time ago.

## The Gauger's Song

Ah a gauger now in Dublin at the time that I was there,
He fancied that a private still it was being worked somewhere.
He met me out one morning, perhaps he fancied that I knew,
But I didn't know him at all, at all, saying, 'Pat how do you
    do?'

'I'm pretty well your honour but allow me for to say,
I don't know you at all, at all.' Said he, 'Perhaps you may,
I want to find a something out, assist me if you will,
This fifty pounds if you can tell me where there's a private
    still.'

'Gimme the fifty pounds,' said I, 'and faith I surely can,
As you may depend on me as I'm an Irishman.'
The fifty pounds was then laid down, I pocketed the fee,
Sayin', 'Button up your coat old chap, and pad the road with
    me.'

Along the road we quickly walked for miles full half a score,
Till by his pace it was evident his feet were getting sore.
He says, 'How far have we to go for I am getting tired.'
'We'd better take a car,' said I, so a jaunting car we hired.

As soon as we got on the car he says, 'Now tell me, Pat,
Where is this blessed private still, don't take me for a flat?'
'A flat your honour, no,' said I, 'but hear me if you will,
And I will at once tell you where there's a private still.'

'We're coming to it close now,' said I, 'and the barracks close
  at hand,
And if you look straight through the gate, you'll see and
  hear the band;
And when the band's done playing, you will see the soldiers
  drill.'
'Oh never mind the soldiers, tell me where's the private still?'

'In half a minute now,' said I, 'I'll point him out to you.
For there he is the very one standing between them two.'
'Arra who is that you mean?', said he. Said I, 'My brother
  Bill.
They won't make him a corporal, then he's a private still.'

Then the gauger swore and tore his hair 'til have his money
  back,
I jumped upon the car myself and bolted in a crack,
And people as he walked along all much against his will,
Shouted after him, 'Exciseman, did you find the private still?'

But the Bishop was far more effective. They all went by him.
They didn't like the law altogether but like they weren't as afraid
of them as they were of their own clergy.

That was well into the 'thirties when that the priest stopped it.
There was a couple of priests went round them. They thought it
was better for to collect all the utensils that was for making the
drink from the people. I knowed a place where they went round
and got several worms and stills and arms and everything and they
took them away in cars and vans. But there was *an old crater* that
I used to know well, he used to make a sup and many's the time
I got a sup of it myself indeed. He was the name of Jemmy Mahon.
The two clergymen come to him and they explained what they
had come for. They come for his worm and arm and still. He says,
'I'm very sorry, you would be the last men in the world I'd refuse
but these articles was never as busy as now. For I've a wee sup
to make myself and there's a neighbour indeed has asked them

off me no longer ago than last night.' And he says, 'I'm very sorry men if you call back about the week-end I'll tell you what I can do for you!' You see he pretended that the priest was getting the articles to run a sup for themselves.

I called down with Jemmy I used to be in it an odd time – this was of a Sunday evening. I tipped the door and in a wee while Jemmy come to it and opened it. The house was full of smoke and, 'Be God', he says, 'you put the life out of me I thought it was *the boys with the black peaks* but come in and sit down anyway.' He was scraping a wee bit of *lootin* off the arm and the worm, and says I, 'You're getting on rightly Jemmy?' 'Well as you could expect,' he says. 'It's very lucky you happened in you'll help me *to red out*.' So I helped poor Jemmy to red out *the tools*, hide the worm and arm and still. So we went in and sat down and had a few drinks. When Jemmy got a few drinks he started to get over a wee verse or two of a song and this is the version he had:

## The Mountain Dew

Oh grass may grow and waters flow in a free and easy way,
But give me enough of the fine old stuff that's made in
  Granuel.
These gaugers all round Donegal, Galway and Leitrim too,
They will take a slip and they'd have a sip of the real old
  mountain dew.

CHORUS
Ha-tha diddly-al-de-dal, de-de-diddly-al-de-dal, do-de dal dal
  diddly al-de dee.
He diddly-al-de-dal, ha-tha diddly al-de dal, do-de dal dal
  diddly-al-de-dee.

Now all young men that use the pen, has wrote the praises
  high,
Of the sweet poteen from Ireland green, distilled from wheat
  and rye.
Away with pills it can cure all ills, with the pagan, Christian
  or Jew;
So take up your coat and clear your throat, of the real old
  mountain dew.

CHORUS

I believe that was maybe all of that song poor old Jemmy was fit to sing at that time anyway.

People has a great confidence in it for a cure for anything. It was a great cure for a calf or a cow or anything like that, that suddenly took bad. You bottled it to them. I remember one example specially. A boy came running to our door one night. He had a big lump of a calf, you might say it was a heifer, about fifteen or sixteen months old. He said it was very bad, would I come to see it? 'Oh,' I said, 'I will surely.' I went up to see it and it was lying stretched out. You'd think it was going to die and its head flat on the ground and its tongue out. So he says that the calf will die. 'Well', says I, 'it looks very ill anyway or what will we give it?' Says I, 'You've none of the clear stuff about, poteen?' 'Dang but', he says, 'I think I have a wee bottle of it down the road here.' So he went down the road and he was no more than about five or ten minutes away till he come back with this wee bottle. I put a taste of sugar in a mug and about two glasses of this in the mug and stirred it up and put it in a bottle, and I lifted his head and bottled it in slowly. So I says, 'We'll go into the house and sit down now for half an hour to see how it'll get on.' We went out in about half an hour and the calf was lying normal, the way any calf would be. Says I, 'We'll go in again for another wee while till we see how it'll do.' So we went out in another quarter of an hour or so and the calf was chewing its cud, as well as it ever was.

I heard the old people talk about it, that there was a cure in it. That's the reason why I asked this man had he any. I've sung you that one about Tom Kelly's cow haven't I?* It was used as a cure for people too, them that never took it. Them that wouldn't let poteen into the house nor would be afraid of anyone that would make it and still I knowed of them being cured of an illness. Like something like appendicitis. They took bad cramps in their stomach. You wouldn't want to give too much if it was strong poteen. When they weren't used to it they wouldn't want to get more nor a glass, nor they would hardly want to get a glass. If you did drink poteen or was accustomed to it, I don't know whether it'd be effective or not. I can't tell you that, but I knowed of it being effective.

Well they could sing at a wake too you know. I never heard them singing too much in my time. Before it, as far as I heard, they did.

* See p. 17.

Usually when a man died the news spread very much round about the country. The neighbours all came in if he died early in the day and attended what they called the burial house. They stayed there for a certain period of time. They might get some whiskey, or drink a cup of tea, and they left again. It was only to visit the place do you see. So there come in another party at night. Aye at night then there gathered in a fairly big crowd at every house where there was a corpse and they got their pipes put around. Clay pipes they were at that time. There was certain relatives of the deceased would cut the tobacco and bring round the plates and fill their pipes and they'd have a smoke. There might be old women would take a clay pipe too and have a smoke out of it at that time. Some of them would be sitting in *the room*. The corpse would always be in a room in bed. But the rest would be sitting in the kitchen excepting for a few of the relatives. Some neighbours might go up and say a few prayers over the corpse, others didn't. If they were no relations or anything they never left the kitchen. Well everything would be talked over, crops, fairs and markets, and everything like that.

I remember a particular wake. There was an old woman and man lived together, they were brother and sister. This old man took ill and well he only lived for three or four days from he took ill. It must have been the heart or something, for the doctor and clergy had to be called on very sudden. But there was a neighbour of his own and the two used to dispute an odd time you know. They were two big able strong men and they used to have an odd row back and forward. They didn't like each other but still when this man died the other man came into the wake one night. He was in the room along with the relatives and friends and some of them says, 'Yes this was a good old man.'

'He was,' he said, 'surely but me and him disputed.'

'Well he was always too able for you,' says some of the rest of them.

'Oh!', he says, 'he wasn't now.'

But there was young fellows there before this man came in at all, had a wee bit of a rope tied to the corpse's feet. Had it tucked under the chairs. They knowed of course the kind of this man. He was very cross. When they said that he could always have him he said, 'He couldn't have, living or dead.' These parties, as soon as he said that, pulled the cord and the corpse swung up and hit him in the face. He collapsed, fell over with fear and had to be carried out to the street. It was good sport.

At that time they'd play an odd trick but things are very different now altogether. There'd be no singing allowed nor there wouldn't be any tricks played on a corpse now as they did at that time. There's nobody of the relations would let that carry on go at all. At that time they *didn't think a hate of it*. They might laugh at it as hearty as a rank stranger would. They didn't look so sincere on it as they do now. They were a wee bit rougher and they didn't look on it so sincere as they do at the present time.

# On Clyde's bonny banks . . .

I started work after I quit school. I was about twelve years old, and when I was thirteen I went back for a few months in the winter. At that time when you got able to work there was no more school. There was a man beside me used to draw milk to the creamery and I started with him and drew milk for a few months, or maybe twelve. That was to Rosslea. The small creamery there was at it and you supplied that milk and it come right round. They called it *skim* that was let down on the other side and you took that home with you. At that time they fed pigs with it and calves. You took the skim home with you and it took about half a day for to do that work, from about eight o'clock in the morning till about twelve or one. The pay was about four shillings a day.

When you come home if it was in the hay season you helped to make the hay and if it was in the corn season you helped to cut the harvest. You wrought on till whatever time you had light to work.

Well when I was drawing milk to the creamery I used to meet a man the name of Johnston, Samuel Johnston. He used to draw milk to the creamery too. They had a lot of cows themselves and he could nearly load a cart himself. He lived beside Lough Ooney on that estate where Murray and McAdams was drowned, and every day I went he'd come round and he'd say, 'Now take your time John I want you, don't go away till I see you.' So every day he'd get me to sing a verse or two of this song about the two men that was drownded. I suppose I'd be getting on to seventeen, maybe seventeen or eighteen then.

Lough Ooney is between Monaghan and Clones. A very remarkable thing is of Lough Ooney, since them men was drownded, it turns three colours in the one day. In the morning it's red, it turns blue at midday or after it and it turns real black in the afternoon. I have seen it myself. It's past hearsay I know that myself.

The reason why that this man was interested in Murray – his father knew Murray – this gentleman lived in this estate. He was a great gentleman I think right enough now, he and McAdams. Well Murray was a Protestant and McAdams was a Catholic, but they were very chummy and *great* their lifetime. They went to have a sail on this lough on *a cot* one Sunday morning and both of them was drowned.

It'd be a long time ago that I got that song, fifty years indeed. I learned it from an old fellow up beside Lough Ooney. He was the name of Eddie Sweeney. I'll give it to you if I remember it when I start it now:

## Lough Ooney

Oh you bards of this nation, and sons of old Erin,
Come join me in deep consolation,
Since a hero of fame, noble Murray by name,
And a friend 'til our great Irish nation.

Your gods to invoke all their sweets to enjoy,
His spouse was fairer nor Juno.
For the plains of Columba [Columbia] could never compare,
'Til the lovely sweet shades of Lough Ooney.

Around its castle that day there was employment and pay,
For the labourer, the weak and the tradesmen.
Like a hero of fame he supported the game,
And he cheerfully paid the brave sportsman.

He threw open his door, to the aged and poor,
To the lame, weak, the sick and the puny.
He ordered his dear to have cordials prepared,
For to heal the distressed at Lough Ooney.

On last Sunday morning, as Phoebus adorned
And the wee birds they sang so melodious,
Says Murray to McAdams, 'We'll both have a sail,
Since our pleasure-boat's rigged out commodious.'

58

His comrade said, 'Nay, let us tarry that day,'
As the morning seemed both rough and stormy;
But none could persuade as his courage upheld
He must have that sail on Lough Ooney.

So straight to the harbour these heroes did go
As they manfully ploughed the proud billows.
But little they knew, their hours were but few,
That the cold sands would soon be their pillow.

The storm that arose and the billows they roared,
The great waves they dashed in full fury.
Their boat were upset, they were cast over deck,
For to drink at the waves of Lough Ooney.

Brave Murray swam on till he came near the shore,
With the terrible waves covering over him.
He turned on his back thinking the waves they'd get slack,
And expecting new strength 'til recover.

When a man from the shore cries turn no more,
And you will reach harbour full sooner.
He cried, 'I'm undone, and my glass it's nigh run,
Saying adieu to you lovely Lough Ooney'.

Brave McAdams drew nigh 'til the billows passed by,
When he saw his brave comrade was drownded.
He called ways to Job and the Powers above,
But the heavens still seemed to be frowning.

Overwhelmed with grief and could find no relief,
To the morning sun rested at noon-day.
With a struggle he got 'til that same fatal spot,
But he sank to the sands of Lough Ooney.

Now why didn't they stay from the waters that day,
Until that fatal hour would pass over?
But how could they flee from an invited decree
When it was pressed by the goddess of Juno;

And called by that fate till the glorious retreat,
From the lovely sweet shades of Lough Ooney.

It's now to conclude o'er my tragedy's scene,
The celestial waves shone all around them.

With glory no more will the cuckoo be heard,
Or the nightingale sing so melodious.

No more shall them echoes be heard 'til resound,
In the valleys or green woods so bonny.
Since Murray took flight from the ragings of light,
And the lovely sweet shades of Lough Ooney.


Well a couple or three years after the Easter Rising in Dublin
there were troubled times round our country. You never had
peace to go any road and they even had a curfew put on. You see
when the trouble sometimes come on there were a lot of trouble.
They were digging trenches across the road and they were cutting
down trees and there was a lot of trouble getting everywhere at
the time. If you went out of the house you were stopped by
somebody. If it wasn't by soldiers or police it was by IRA or
Republicans. You were stopped by some party anyway and there
wasn't much comfort. So then it come on to be that bad that there
was a curfew on for a period of time. You know it broke out in
1916. The riots broke out in Dublin but then it would be on
further. It would be the 'eighteens or 'nineteens when it would be
curfew time about, or 'twenties maybe. When the curfew come on
you couldn't be seen out of the house after eleven or twelve
o'clock. I think it was twelve o'clock when it started. It come back
to eleven o'clock. Of course young fellows they would run to an
odd dance and go to an odd ceilidh and if you were too late you
got into trouble. You might get into jail if you were caught being
out after hours when the curfew was on. I remember coming
along one night from old Paddy's house, Paddy McMahon's. I
was coming across the fields, me and another young fellow the
name of McCabe, and just as we were crossing the road this light
shone on us. It was a lorry load of what they called *the Black and
Tans*. So they bid to see a shadow of us crossing the road and we
lay down in *the sheough* going across the field, but they come in.
We set out across country home to beat them. They went round
the road of course. They were listening, I suppose, and flashing
their lights and we had to run past our own house to get clear.
They tapped at the door and everywhere but they went away again,
done no harm.
They put the curfew on because times went that bad you see.

These men, what you call the IRA or Republicans, they were digging trenches and putting bushes across the road, ambushing them and shooting the soldiers from both sides. When they got them to come to this place where they had the bush across they attacked them on both sides and killed a lot of soldiers. That's what caused them to bring on curfew. If you were found out after it you were liable to be shot. There was nobody caught about our side. It kept fairly quiet only just that you wouldn't want to be out. These Crossley Tenders and all was going the roads, at all hours of the night.

Well you see as it is, I suppose maybe there's some of it going on today. The Catholics would maybe go and if they knowed of a prominent man being busy with these English soldiers or anything they went and maybe burned his house. There was retaliation then, they would come and burn a Catholic house. So it never stopped until it went as far as the towns, and you might say that wee village beside us in Rosslea it was burned to the ground. It would be twenty-one or thereabouts. The Protestant people spilt petrol on the houses, on the Catholic houses all, and burned them out nearly every one of them. There was a song about it I think, but I haven't any of it.*

There was some very vicious things done you know after Rosslea was burned. There was a man in our country he lived a wee short distance out of Rosslea. He was the name of Nixon. So he was supposed to carry the petrol which burned the Catholic houses. He was supposed to be, I couldn't tell whether he did or not. But they went to his house, the Sinn Feiners and Republicans – they were called Volunteers at that time. The Volunteers went to the house and ordered him out. He didn't come out so they fired in and he fired out, as long as he had ammunition and the way of working. So when it was done he come out and surrendered, but they shot him anyway. The wife she tried to save him. She came out after him and she tried to save him and keep them back from firing. She put up her hands and they blew two fingers off. So that was a very vicious thing.

Of course there was a retaliation of all these things. There was a lot of Catholics shot after that and put into jail, and there was a lot of them got out of the country to America and Australia, 'til all over the globe.

* See Appendix 2, song 55.

So there wasn't much comfort and apart from that there wasn't so much work about the country and the wages were very bad. So I decided that I'd go to Scotland to look for a job. So, I went out, and at that time it wasn't too dear for to get to Scotland. I booked my way at Clones to the north of Scotland. That's about one hundred and fifty or two hundred miles off the Central Station in Glasgow, that's twenty-one shillings right through. I'd say that was in between 'eighteen and 'twenty.

My mother didn't want me to go, but she didn't mind when it was my own pleasure do you know. Edward had been away at that time 'til Blantyre outside Glasgow. I didn't even go to him at that time. I went to the north of Scotland where there was a tunnel from a place they called Fairset to Fort William. I think it was for water, maybe for aluminium works, in a place they called Kinlochleven. Well I travelled out there, me and another comrade the name of McCabe. We got the train down to Belfast here, walked down to the docks, got on the boat and sailed into Glasgow, went to Central Station and got an express train right through to Fairset, the place where the job started. The minute we got off the train, we had about half a mile to walk up the railway, this neighbour of mine Tommy Lyttle, he was a funny kind of fellow, anyway he never was beat for an answer. He was shovelling clay down. Och! a mound as big as a house where he was shovelling. It was a big job shovelling down altogether. I said you're working hard Tommy. 'I believe,' he said, 'that this place would all go wrong if I left!' So we talked to Tommy for a wee while there and we went up to the boss. Sure it wasn't too hard to get a job at that time. He said we could start. Tommy explained the thing to him. He said, 'These two young fellows is looking for a job', the minute we went up and we got started right away next morning. It was digging clay and throwing it in with a shovel into these what they called skips. It run down a narrow gauge on four wheels and we cooped it. You always wrought fairly hard now to keep yourself warm, for it was a cold place. It was coming on to the winter, it was the month of October and it was blowy and cold out there at that time.

The hours was from eight in the morning till five o'clock in the evening for six days. Well on Saturday you got stopping at twelve o'clock. I was getting from fifty shillings to three pound, according if you wrought a wee little overtime. Fifty shillings was your flat wage. You had to stay in these huts. There might be fifty men in every hut and there'd be five or six of them huts, maybe ten of them all up the line. There'd be a hut here we'd say and another mile of ground there'd be two or three other huts there, and there'd be three or four huts on another mile of ground. These huts were put up by the company that took the contract, but they were very poor huts now, they weren't put too well together. There were splits out between the boards till they were got sealed. They were made of boards, all wood, and felt on the roof of them. Some of them there was corrugated iron put on them, or asbestos after, but at this time that I was out there, there was nothing only felt just across the boards. There was neither toilet or anything else. There was a washhand basin in the corner of the hut that you could wash your hands and you had to have your own towel and other material with you. So the conditions wasn't too good now. They were very cold and the windows were small and there were about fifty or sixty in every hut, single beds.

When the frost got fairly heavy you know it was terrible at that time. I remember we were leaving down the foundation for these pugs, small engines for to run up to bring the stuff from one camp to the other – they called them pugs. I saw me and a wee fellow they called Cormiskey from the Gorbal's Cross in Glasgow, we were carrying *rathes* and the iron it'd stick to your hand. If your spittle happened to drop on the collar of your coat it's be *a spicket* before you'd knock it off. And I saw me, before they got the huts fixed up right in that place, before they sealed these creases between the wood, lying up against the wood. And I saw my hair being freezed out through it, and having to take my two hands to pull it in in the morning.

There was a hotplate in the middle of the floor for cooking your food. A big square thing, well fifteen or twenty could stand round it and forty or fifty pans could be on it. It was big. The company supplied the coal but you had your own pans and your own mugs, and you bought everything out of the shop. You had to go to the canteen to buy your food and you cooked your own meals on the hotplate. Things wasn't that dear now at that time. You could go to the canteen and you could get your whole week's provisions for ten shillings and you could be fairly well fed at that. You'd have bacon, sausages, bread, tea and everything for about ten shillings, and there was plenty of people done with far less, seven and six and eight shillings.

There was a brave few from about Clones and Monaghan too at this work, but the majority of them there was a whole lot from Donegal now. At night there was a lot of them playing cards. Some of them had a game of this dice as they called them 'lucky old crown and anchor'. They bet very heavy on that, any of these men that had money, either *higgins* or gaffers on the jobs. Some played dominoes. There wasn't a pub near us. The nearest was Fort William and that was a long road down. It'd be the big end of twenty mile. There would be some singing, but there was very little men that did sing there. I never heard any except an old fellow; he was an aged man the name of Miller. He used to sing an odd song about the coal mines. He had a song about a coal disaster near 'dark Lochnagar', but at that time I would get it very tight to understand him because he was what they called a Highlander. I wasn't interested in it anyway you know. It was a different kind of a song and he had a different way of singing it. I had a snatch of one of his songs now concerning a disaster. It'd be the same as the Blantyre disaster,* but he had a different way you see.

## The Handsome Collier Lad

My love he is a collier lad, he works all underground,
His modest mild behaviour is nowhere can be found;
His dark blue eyes, his curly hair, and cheeks of a rosy red,
But alas my handsome collier lad, he's numbered with the
    dead.

Last night when I lay on my bed, the moon was shining clear,
I heard a cry of murder, whilst dreaming of my dear.
As he laid his head down on my breast the blood flowed like
    a stream,
And with a cry I wakened and found it was a dream.

But the very next morning early my dreams were satisfied,
The neighbours gathered around me, your true love's dead
    they cried.
While he bein' at his work last night the roof on him did fall,
Oh the woe and sorrow at my heart I could to no one tell.

* See p. 69.

For the ring was bought, the day was fixed, when married we
  would be,
My love and I for to set sail bound for Amerikey.
To push along our fortune, all on some foreign shore,
But alas my handsome collier lad I never will see more.

The summer-time will come again, when all things will be gay,
The little birds they'll frisk about and the lambs'll sport and
  play.
Sure you'll be glad when I'll be sad, all with a constant mind,
Here's a health to every collier lad that works down the mine.

I stayed in the north of Scotland now for about fifteen or
eighteen months. The place had got very lonely. There was
nothing there only work and sleep and there wasn't much for a
young fellow them days. I had a brother in Blantyre, his name was
Edward, so I moved down to him and I got started a few days
after it along with him in the pit. Us two was what they called
brushers. In a coal mine it is complicated. When the colliers
shovelled out the coal into the pans the rock was to be taken off
above to leave people liberty to walk in a road. You put wood on
both sides to keep the wall up and bored a six-foot drill and fired
a shot and stowed the rock in to both sides. There was a fireman
for that. When you had the hole bored he put in the gelignite,
or whatever you called it and he fired the shot himself.

There were some accidents happened in the pits when I worked
there. I remember one time that the shaft was closed, the cages
had stuck in it and the cable rope had broken. So there was a fall
at the face and the fireman came in and told us that we couldn't
get out for the cage being stuck and we had to go out an airway.
It was a place for air getting out about two foot, or hardly it, wide.
It went on in a slope for about two mile, or two mile and a half.
So we had to creep out one after the other. Creep out as well as we
could, lying on our tummy crawling away till we got out. It took
us about two hours, or two hours and a half I suppose. We got
out to the surface all right, but we were surely like colliers when we
got out that length.

I remember another time we were coming out *the road* me and
another fellow, his name was William Armstrong. He was in front
of me. There was a cable-rope run along the bottom of the hutches

that would bring them out, and times the cable-rope would be lying flat on the ground. The hutches was like wee square boxes for carrying the coal. There might be five or six of them always on that cable-rope, coming in to the face to take out the coal. They were on a rail. So when the hutches would be full the cable-rope would tighten, it would spring up maybe a foot, or a foot and a half, sometimes two. So he happened to put his foot on it. He was walking on the side of the sleepers that was under *the gauge*, so he put his foot on this cable-rope just when it was rising and it struck him, against his head, against an iron girder above. So he died instantly.

The work wasn't too bad. The worst frightening, leaving the odd accident, you'd get would be the first time you'd get in the cage and go down three or four, or six hundred fathom down. You got a speedy drop but it frightened you then the first time you went down, but you never thought a bit about it afterwards. We wrought there five days a week and our lunch we brought it down with us. A flask and *a piece* in what they called a piece-box. We took that when we were working about three hours and we wrought an eight-hour day. Our pay at that time was about £3 10s. 0d. or £3 12s. 0d. I started work in the pits about 1924 and wrought there till 1926 when the big collier strike came. When the big strike came on all left. Union men ordered them to leave and push for higher pay. That strike lasted for sixteen weeks. So it was a very hard time, hard to get work anywhere.

I got a job with a building company across the Clyde, in a place then called Bothwell. Lucky enough I got it in the second week, but there was other men, thousands of them, had a very bad time. They couldn't get work, was just unlucky enough not to get it. There wasn't much, at that time, could be done about it. There was no *Bureau* nor nothing. You had whatever few shillings *the Parish* gave you to live on and it was very light, five or six shillings a week. It was not good enough to support you so they went out in crowds day and night both. In fact one day I did see them breaking into shops and taking out food and sometimes some of them would break into a public house and take some drink too. The police had a lot of trouble with them and they were terrible hard to control betimes, because there was a lot of them nearly starving. So that continued on – when the strike was on a month or so till the sixteen

66

weeks was over – till they started work again. They got a pay rise, what they thought was a good one, a pound a week. At that time it was very good.

Well when I was on that job about a week I asked the foreman could he start another man and he said maybe he could. So my brother got started too and we both continued on working for a long time. I was attending the bricklayers – carrying a hod on my shoulder with twelve bricks in it, mixing mortar and cement and sand and bringing a hod of it up to the bricklayers too. I wrought five days of the week and Saturday till twelve o'clock. It was an eight-hour day and you started at eight o'clock. I had almost four pounds for that work.

Well this place in Blantyre was more enjoyable than the north of Scotland because you had a lot of friends. Every night you could go out to see them and there was a club up the road. We used to go to it and play cards and dominoes and draughts and have an odd pint of beer and a talk. You had plenty of comrades and there was a better life.

There used to be a fellow the name of Paddy McMahon he was a neighbour of my own. He was in Blantyre too and he was a very jolly kind of fellow, fond of a drink and fond of dancing and singing particularly. He was great company to be along with and no matter where he went and how bad the times was Paddy could nearly get a job any road. That time of the big strike he was going down the line and there was a fellow sinking drains for sewerage. So Paddy said for the joke of it, not thinking he'd get a job, 'Could you give me a start?' 'Och!' he says, 'I couldn't I'm full up.' So Paddy says, 'You could've started me and busted yourself.' Paddy was a few yards down the road and he called him back. 'Come here,' he says, 'Paddy!' They called every Irishman Paddy of course. He started Paddy there and then and there was no such thing as getting a job any road. I used to ceilidh to Paddy's house when Paddy wasn't very old either. He was a little older than me. He was fond of hunting and dancing and nearly every one of them in the house – there was five or six of them – they all could play a fiddle or a flute, or they could step-dance or something.

Anytime I ever met Paddy in Blantyre we'd always have a drink. He was a great man for asking for songs and he'd sing a song himself. He had an old song that I remember about the Bridge Fair, and he used to often sing that when he'd be in company.

## The Maid of the Colehill

It being on the seventh of January when go'ng to the 'Bridge
Fair
I met a bonnie lassie, combed down her yellow hair.
The a-more that I did gaze on her my heart with love did fill,
She's my beauty's bright, my heart's delight, she's the maid
of the Colehill.

I had no mind to tarry long when I left home that day,
I had no mind to tarry long when I left Lisnaskea,
But meeting with some friends of mine when I arrived there,
So kindly they saluted me and said you're welcome to the
fair.

We then went into a Public House where there we all sat
down,
The jugs of punch came tumbling and the toast went merrily
round.
The liquor it was plenty, and we drank with a free goodwill,
Here's a flowing glass to the blooming lass, she's the maid of
the Colehill.

Some people please to tell me that my love she does me slight,
But when I'm in her company, I think all things are right.
She says herself she'll marry me and that with a free goodwill,
She'll forsake her friends and relations and likewise the
Colehill.

I just remember – it's like a kind of a dream – that we were in
a public house, the name of Malcolm's in Blantyre, and there
were four or five of us there. So Paddy asked a couple of these
men had they 'The Blantyre Explosion', that song. We had a lot
of drink taken the same night and I can't call to memory right,
but I think three of them sung it at least. So Paddy was sitting up
in the corner, on a high stool with a pint in his hand, and he'd
shake his head at me every time that they'd sing the song, these
three one after the other. They all had different ways of it and in
fact maybe different airs. Some of them had different airs so far
as I can mind. But Paddy says to me, 'You sing that John.' So I

sung it and I could see him smiling all the time. 'Well,' he says, 'if any of the rest of you is asked to sing "The Blantyre Explosion" say, "No, sir, I can't." John's is the right version of it. You hear it and you know it as well as I do.' Poor old Paddy he's living in Belfast yet and he likes to hear this 'Blantyre Explosion' yet. So I'll give you a verse of it now.

## The Blantyre Eplosion

Oh on Clyde's bonny banks where I lately did wander,
To the village of Blantyre where I chanced to stray,
I espied a young woman, was dressed in deep mourning,
So sadly lamenting the fate of her love.

I boldly stepped to her, said I, 'My poor woman,
Come tell me the cause of your trouble and woe,
I do hear you lamenting the fate of some young man,
His name and what happened him I'd like for to know.'

Well sighing and sobbing she at length then made answer,
'John Murphy, kind sir, was my true lover's name.
Twenty-one years of age, and modest good behaviour,
To work in the mines of High Blantyre he came.'

On the eleventh of December I long will remember,
In health and in strength 'til his labour did go;
But on that fatal morning without one moment's warning,
Two hundred and ten in cold death did lie low.

There was fathers and mothers, there was widows and orphans,
In stone field High Blantyre where hundreds do mourn.
There was old aged parents for their sons they loved dearly,
By that sad explosion will never return.

But they say it's not right for the dead to be grieved,
There's nothing but trouble bestowed upon me.
He's gone from this world, but a short time before me,
In hopes to rejoin him in sweet unity.

The spring it'll come with the flowers of summer,
That blows through its wildness so lovely and fair,
I will gather the snowdrops, primroses and daisies,
Round my true lover's grave I will transplant them there.

Well I learned that song from an old man, he was a Highlander.
He was in the club one Sunday evening and he sung it. I don't
know his name mind you. I might have known it at the time but
I forget his name. So I got him to sing it the second time and I
picked it up. It was supposed to be the right version of 'The
Blantyre Explosion', for he wrought in that pit the shift before the
explosion happened. He was just only up out of it the night before.

Aye, there's another song that I learned off a fellow. He came
from this country first but he wrought a long time about Edinburgh.
It was at a wedding in Renfrew Street in Glasgow. The fellow was
getting married, he was a Robert McManus and we were at the
wedding. So this McCormick fellow, that was working in Edinburgh, he sung this song. It was 'The Blooming Caroline from
Edinburgh Town'.

## Blooming Caroline from Edinburgh Town

Oh ye blythesome lads and lassies attend until my fame,
It's of a beautiful fair one, was hastened in her prime.
Her cheeks they were a rosy red admired by all around,
And they called her blooming Caroline from Edinburgh Town.

Young Henry being a Highland lad a-courting her he came,
But when her parents came to know they were angry at the
    same.
Young Henry being offended and until her did say,
'Rise up my blooming Caroline and we will run away.'

'Oh we will go to London, to London with great speed,
And when that we're in London we'll live happy there indeed.'
She gathered up her costly robes and the stars came tripping
    down,
And away went blooming Caroline from Edinburgh Town.

They were not long in London, oh scarce a half a year
When hard-hearted Henry on her did prove severe.
'I'm bound for seas my darling your parents did on me
    frown,
So make no delay but beg your way to Edinburgh Town.'

This maid in grief without relief until the woods are gone,
To eat what fruit as she will find, all on the bushes growin';

For some takes pity on her and others will on her frown,
And some will say, 'What made you stray from Edinburgh
    Town!'

She leaned her back until an oak and she began to cry,
Just watching the small boats and ships on sea as they
    passed by.
She gave three cheers on Henry, 'Why did you on me frown,
Don't you mind the day we stole away from Edinburgh
    Town?'

Her bonnet and cloak, likewise a note, she left upon the
    shore,
And in this note the lines were wrote, 'Alas I am no more.
I'm in the deep and is fast asleep where small fish does swim
    round.
I was once the blooming Caroline from Edinburgh Town.'

There's that song too about a boy that got a hair-cut from a
barber in Glasgow and I got it from a fellow the name of McManus.
I was at his wedding in Renfrew Street in Glasgow. He had been
in Glasgow from he was a boy. So he's still alive and working
and this is the version of the song. My brother Brian sings this
too.*

## The Glasgow Barber

When first I sailed over from Belfast to Greenock,
My blood felt congealed I was leaving the sod.
My heart swelled as big as the cot I sailed o'er on,
When the gaffer had refused to give Paddy a job.

I landed in Glasgow, inquired for Queen Street,
Called into a barber he bid me sit down.
He placed me real fair in the arms of a chair
And he covered me o'er with his grandmother's gown.

Says he, 'Is it shaving?' I says, 'Are you raving?
It's the hair on me head I want cut in a row;
Before you'd be going I'd like you'd be knowing
It's the style that we have in the County Mayo.'

* See *Folksongs Sung in Ulster*, Mercier Press, 1970, song 30.

Well he placed a steel clinker above my eye winker,
You'd have swore it was the ramps of Moll Brannigan's fan.
He oiled it and sleeked it, he combed it and streaked it,
He oiled front and rear with his two little hands.

He says, 'Irish Pat you'll pay fourpence for that,
It's a cut that an Irishman seldom do show.
It's the ladies conceit, aye and ne'er will you greet
When you land with your friends in the County Mayo.'

'Bad winds dear soul do you think I'm a loobey?
Oh hell to your soul sure the hair was me own;
And before I'd make bargain with the landlords of Scotland,
I'd rather make bargain with the landlords at home.'

He called in two bobbies for to take Irish Paddy,
With hats on their heads like large rucks of straw,
Says they, 'toramusha', I says, 'arra-gusha!'
It's a word that we use in the County Mayo.

Well they took to their batons, I took to me stick,
And the police and barber I soon did take down.
I left them a mark for to buy sticking plasters,
And I straight took my way to the east of the town.

When I looked in the glass you'd 'a swore I was an ass,
My lugs stood so high and my head it hung low.
Bad luck to his tristles, his bells and steam whistles
And hurrah for the girls in the County Mayo.

Well there's another song I think it's a kind of Scotch song. I learned it from a fellow that come out of America the name of Cadden. He sung it when he came home on holiday and I picked it up from him.

## The Bonnie Wee Lassie that Never Said No

Oh you folks of this nation of high and low station,
All you wee lasses give ear to my song;
If you listen a while it'll cause you to smile;
It's not my intention to keep you too long.
At a crossroads as I passed sure I met a wee lass,

And I asked her if she'd be quite willing to go,
Take share in a gill, she says, 'Yes sir, I will.
For I'm the wee lassie that never said no!'

To an ale-house we went where some money I spent,
And I called on a dram and cigar for to smoke.
The waiter came in with a bottle of gin,
He says, lassie be mindful and humour the joke.
For the beer and the whiskey we drank is so frisky,
And kisses in dozens on herself I bestowed.
I says, 'My delight, can we tarry all night?'
She says, 'I'm the wee lassie that never said no!'

Now the landlady thinking we were slow in drinking,
She opened the door and walked in with a smile,
With great freedom there she drew up her chair,
Oh she was the queen that could swig it in style.
The beer and the whiskey we drank is so frisky
I says, 'It's near time to our hammock we'd go.'
'All right come away but the reckoning first pay,
For I'm the wee lassie that never said no!'

The reckoning I paid and the landlady said,
'There is two and six still left for your bed.'
I popped it right down my little half-crown
When she saw my purse to the lassie she said,
'You should take in a dram for to treat this young man
To cheer up his spirits because they are low.'
'It's that I will do bring a bottle for you,
For I'm the wee lassie that never said no!'

That bottle came in of the best Holland Gin,
And I was resolved right sober to keep.
But glass after glass did merrily pass,
To the lass and the landlady both fell asleep.
Twelve pounds then I took out of her pocket book,
I says, 'It's near time I would bundle and go,
Good-night maid,' said I, but there was no reply
For the bonny wee lass was too drunk to say no.

I scampered away to the town of Rosslea
Where I met a few lads that belonged to the 'crew'

73

They laughed at the fun when they heard what I'd done,
For I up and told them of all I came through.
Into Flynn's then we went where some money I spent,
And I never cried halt till the cocks they did crow.
And the devil the one glass did I ever let pass,
But I drank to the wee lass that never said no.

I didn't see many *ballad-singers* in the streets of Scotland but I
saw good music men. I remember one evening, in the village of
Blantyre, coming up from my work. I had been washing my face
at the window and this fellow come along. He was a tall, light man
and he was playing a fiddle. So it was lovely music, I thought I
never heard the like of it. I went to the window and whatever I
had in my pockets, coppers or silver, I give them to him anyway
for I was that much interested in his music, and he went round
every door like that. So as soon as I got washed up and got a bit
of dinner and a wee cup of tea I followed on and he was in a wee
place they called Springwells then. So I listened to him playing
there and he was getting bags of money. There was a wee boy
along with him was holding the cap and he used to have to
empty it into a little satchel he had like a schoolbag, every town
or village he'd go into. I followed him on to Hamilton, and he
played at every door nearly there. Through Motherwell and into
Wishart and it was late bed-time when I got back. He was from
County Tyrone here, but I never got his name. He was the
loveliest player I ever listened to.

Well I worked in that job with my brother for ten or twelve
months. I was tired of Scotland because the money wasn't that
great and the work was hard enough. I left Scotland then and came
home to my mother's place at Follom Big. So I wrought on the
farm for a year or so and then we took contracts, me and my
brother, repairing the roads. The County Council always put
tenders in the paper for the roads. There'd be maybe three or
four mile of a road, or five or six mile of a road. Some of them
was shorter, two mile of a road, and you put in a tender for what
you thought you could do it at, so the lowest tender then got it.
So you had to keep these roads for three years. Repair them every
three months and you had to raise the stones in the quarry, of
course. It was a tumbling quarry we wrought in. There was gravel
and stones both in it. This wasn't a 'rock' we wrought in, there

was big stones in it and small stones and actually gravel. You could screen gravel in it too, for the road. They called it a tumbling quarry because you had to screen the gravel up against a bank-ment, for 'til purify it and take the sand out of it and have the gravel by itself. They called it screening it, throwing it up against the bank, the same as you'd throw it up against that wall there and let it tumble down again. The sand would stick there and the gravel would come out by itself, on the bottom. A 'rock' is a solid mountain of stones, the 'rock' was the solid rock. We drew the stones out to a place they called *the new line* that come from Enniskillen to Rosslea. We put so many yards out there and got the stone-breaker and broke, and put them in the potholes in these roads, and grassed the sides of the road in the November quarter with spades. At that time in all, we had four wee roads. There was about ten or eleven mile roughly. We might get from £10 to £12 a quarter for every road.

The roads was in a bad condition, some of them, for there hadn't been too much done on them for a period before it. It took a lot of stuff for to do them, and in fact in some places you had to sheet them with broke stones altogether, where part of it'd be low or bad. But the traffic at that time wasn't too heavy. It was just a horse and cart or a donkey and cart. They rumpled down them stones after a time and the road got fairly level and the surface got gooder when you put plenty of stuff on, but there was no tarring or anything at that time at all.

I remember working beside a school, they called it Rateen School, and the children came down and I told them 'The Penny-worth O'Lies' and they used to torture me afterwards to hear 'The Tuppenceworth O'Lies'. I told them I'd tell them 'The Tup-penceworth O'Lies' the next day. They used to torture me. It was great to see how interested they were listening to 'the Penny-worth O'Lies'. They'd rather hear that as the truth.

Last night about three weeks ago I received a letter from an old Hag's death. And I was that much overcome with grief that every tear that fell from the back of my neck split seven fathoms of a turf bank, or set a mill a-going. I put my two shin bones in my pocket and my head under my arm and I started for seventy-two miles of a walk, walking through banks of stirabout and bogholes of buttermilk till I met an old

75

coachman. He was driving thirty-six dead jack-asses loaded
with empty match-boxes and drinking tea till they were as
black as snow in the face. I asked him did he know where
John Maxwell lived. He told me he did, that he lived on a
high hill down in a low valley where the cock never crew nor
the wind never blew. I went on till I got to John Maxwell's
house and he brought me out to see his eldest son thrashing
peas under *a noggin*. One of these peas jumped over a paper-
stone wall eleventy-seven storey high, and killed a dead dog
that was barking at a pock-marked cat that was knitting
stockings for herself. He brought me then to see some more
of his wonders. Five of his children playing hide-and-go-seek
under *a lap of hay* made of stones . . .

That's just what I remember of it now. There wasn't so much
more, not a great deal. I got it from a man the name of Paddy
Caddan. He had all these old songs and such things as them lies,
and he used to have Catholic songs and Protestant, as he would
call them 'Papishes' and the 'Orangemen' and he had every kind.
Do you know I often thought he was a lost man and that the people
was sleeping at that time that didn't learn all his old ones. That
was the only 'lie' I ever heard. Apparently that was lies enough for
one part of the country!

I was saving money at that time for them years and I gave some
to the house too, for the upkeep of the house. Then this man, his
name was Fox, came home out of England. He was a tradesman
and he was building a byre for about thirty cows at a missionary
college. It was a place they called Shrigley Park outside Burlington.
He asked me if I'd come with him to help him, as the missionary
college people asked him if he could get anybody in that country
that could come along. When I was working there a short time,
I was only about six months or maybe seven working, when I
happened an accident. I was brought to Macclesfield General
Infirmary and I lay there for sixteen weeks.

This was an old estate that these missionaries bought and there
was heavy spouting and a swan's-neck above that led the water
down into the spouting. So I was putting an under joint on it and
when I was driving the rivet the swan's-neck came down on my
head. It was fourteen and a half pounds weight and it split my
head open. So I lay for sixteen weeks in Macclesfield General

Infirmary. I got my wages all the time too and the insurance company paid for the hospital. You see I was stamping my card at the time, which everyone wasn't stamping.

Well when I got this knock on the head you know I was unconscious for a week or ten days. My heart had apparently stopped when I got the bat on the head with the old swan's-neck. The Doctor blew some strychnine into me to start the heart a-going again. So when I put in them sixteen weeks in Macclesfield General Infirmary the Doctor allowed me to come home and have a breath of my own air. Well I got home, my head wasn't so bad but my stomach was still badly affected. It was for two or three years I wasn't fit to do hardly anything, my stomach was very bad. Apparently the Doctor said it was the strychnine that they blew into me that bid to be affect my stomach.

So I doctored for long while in this country. At the latter end, when I had everything tried out, I was in the chemist shop getting some stuff to see would it settle my stomach. So there was an old Yankee fellow in it beside the counter, and when he saw me getting the stuff he stood at the door and he says, 'That's no use at all.'

Says I, 'Why?'

'I'm telling you,' he says, 'I heard you telling the chemist man there that it was your stomach was bad but get a taste of spring water and take the yolk out of an egg and drop the rest of the egg into the spring water and drink it every morning before your breakfast.'

So it was the first cure I got for my stomach. I *never found it* after it. You know at that time there was cures for a lot of things, for such a thing they used to call heart failure. I remember an old girl in our country the name of McCaffrey, from Errisalla, she had a cure for heart failure. You went to her and she put oaten meal in a cup and she went round you three times and said some prayers. I know of a lot she cured of the heart in this way.

I remember another old man in our country, I went to see him myself. I got a bad sprain in the knee – stepped across a ditch and slipped off a stone and strained it badly – and it was that bad that my knee was swelled and it was busting the trousers before I got crippling up to the house. So I was lifted up on a pony by my brother and I went to this man for the cure. He was supposed to have the cure of a strain. When I got that length, it was a nice

77

warm summer's day, and he was sitting on *the landing stone* in front of the house. So he asked me if I was fit to get down off it. I says, 'If I can get any wee help I can.' So he come and I put my hand on his shoulder and got down. He tied the horse to a gate-post and told me to sit down on the landing stone. So he started to rub down the knee and say some prayers that he said, but he pulled every toe three times and rubbed the knee again and said some prayers. So I was able to get on the horse and come home and the swelling went down that night and the next day it was perfect.

There's another cure that I know, that I've used recently myself. For some of my family took *the jaundies* and you had to go to the Jaundy Well, this was the cure. You had to go to the Jaundy Well for the water and when you filled the bottle of water you had to cork it under the water. So you can't speak to nobody till you'd come back home again with it to the patients that had the jaundies. So I've been at it on two occasions last week.\* At this well, where you lift the water, you have to bring a garment of their clothing, or an old sock or stocking or anything, and leave it at the well, hung on a bush. When you come home with it you have to make them drink it in three times, that is inside twenty-four hours. So it has worked very well on two of them so far anyway. You see if you get this cure in time they won't get yellow with the jaundies. But I have a son, Hugh, he had it for a week before he knowed what it was so he's eyes had got yellow. He had taken it then and I understood what it was and I got the water just in time for her. His wife didn't get yellow at all, she got better of it. I've knowed about this Jaundy Well for years and years. Thousands and thousands of people goes to it, in fact I know of this water being taken to Monaghan Hospital to patients in it and it cured them. It's just between Monaghan and Clones on that Monaghan road, a place called Stonebridge.

Anyway, as I said, when I was home a short while I got to be in middling form. My stomach was very bad, so I bought a wee place of my own and set up in it and stayed in it ever since. That was my idea all along, I just intended to settle in my own country.

\* October 1970.

# Now, when that we were married . . .

Well, when I got well again, of course, I decided that I would have a wee home of my own and not be staying with my brother, for he had the farm at home. Brian was older than me and he was entitled to the farm at home and he got it from my mother. So there went a little farm up for auction and at the auction it was going at a very bad price. So the man that was selling it didn't decide to take it anyway. I had been ceilidhing in this house on many's the occasion and knowed the man well. His name was Jimmy Scott and we come to an agreement about the price of the land, so there and then I bought the farm off him. Well this was about a twenty-four or five acre farm and wasn't in good shape when I bought it, but it was going a wee little rough you know, with rushes and the sheoughs wasn't cleaned and it wasn't in very good trim. The house wasn't in good trim either, nor very little out-houses. So I bought it off him that night, when we were talking, at a couple of hundred pounds, owing to the condition the land was in at the time. It was a fair good price for it owing to the prices of other farms was going. That was on Sunday night so we finished up and me and Jimmy went to Clones and squared up for it the next day with a solicitor. It was about two or three months after that I moved in, in the month of July about thirty-seven.

When I bought this farm off Jimmy Scott I decided to get married and settle down in this place. Before that I hadn't thought of it. Her name was Mary Cosgrove and she was living with her father at Errasallagh, up near Newtownbutler there. After I came home out of England I was ceilidhing in the house that my wife came from. I might be in it two or three nights a week and we come into conversation and then we might meet at a dance or a hall and I would go home with her. We decided after a short time for to get married when I bought the place. That was in the month of March and we got married in July. I think it was in thirty-seven, if I'm not mistaken. We just decided among ourselves, I didn't approve of *the matchmaking*. I wouldn't think, if you didn't know one another before that, that the marriage might be a happy one. If you knowed nothing about other, only somebody cut out the thing themselves for you, it would be very unpleasant wouldn't it? She had a stack of money surely and brought plenty of things from home, some furniture and chairs and tables and one thing and another like that that she had to spare, but it wasn't a match.

I heard so many funny stories about the matchmaking in our country. There was one man in particular, just mention no names now, but the one I bought the farm off they used to call him the 'matrimonial agent', and his old father said that he could get a woman for every man in the country and he couldn't get one for himself. Of course you had nothing to do, he was willing to do all that, you didn't need pay for it nor nothing. If he thought that a man wanted a woman, for to keep house for him or anything like that, he went to that man and he asked him would he be agreeable if he brought this girl. And of course if he replied yes, he went to her and he asked her would she agree to take that man, and of course if she did well and good, and if she didn't there could be nothing done about it. If she agreed to take him the wedding come off shortly. At that time you know, if it was the matchmaking, it didn't occur usually with young people do you know. In my time anyway I never saw it, but I did see it in people grown up, with the older generation. Excepting you had a house and *a place* you barely ever looked for a woman, or inquired about one. There was a lot of people would be too shy to go out to look after a woman and they'd get this Jimmy Scott to go to the girl and ask her if she'd take this man. Well you know there's plenty of people that don't get married. Even there's a matchmaker gets a woman for them they can't get married because the father still holds control of the farm. As the saying is, he holds the rein all the time till the boy is too old to think of getting married. So that was one cause that I always thought that kept people from it. I seen an instance in our own country of it, just not within a mile of round us. The father surely wouldn't give the place to the boy and he was too willing, as I knowed myself, for to marry. He wouldn't give the place till he was about forty years of age and

maybe over it, and when he come till that stage the notion of
marrying had went off him, and he never married.

There's several reasons, of course, why people don't get married
even. As a fellow in our country said, there was 'matrimonial
agents' everywhere to get them together. One mightn't be very
handsome looking, the boy or the girl. It's like the song. I got it
from a wee fellow the name of McCluskey from Clones when we
were singing a few songs in a house one night. It was about a
man had a daughter. She wasn't too handsome looking and he
was trying to get her married by means of publishing her property,
all she had. Of course he was telling the truth about her as
well.

## Dick Mooney's Daughter

My name is Dick Mooney, I'm now just a-dying,
I have but one daughter is wanting a man.
It is my intention her fortune to mention,
To get her a husband as soon as I can.
A house and a garden, a snug little farm,
Three cows that are tied that her grandmother sent,
And an old breeding mare, she's blind I declare,
She'll be thirty years old at the first of next Lent.

A byre and a barn, likewise a long stable
With hog house and dog house all set in a range
And a sow and nine young ones that was thick with the measles
And sheep, half a dozen that's black with the mange.
Ten geese and a gander like any commander,
Who rules all the fowl in the great farm yard,
And a big turkey cock, he's the flower of the flock,
He's as proud as a hielander marching on guard.

Her dress in the fashion I mean for to mention,
The latest it cost me a dozen of pounds.
With six gowns of muslin and three rows of flouces,
Her equal are not in this country all round.
A Leghorn bonnet, likewise a grey beaver,
With ribbons and stockings of red, white and green,
And a second-hand spencer to fit her out neatly
With boots, shoes and sandals that's fit for a queen.

Her squeezers in fashion, I pray don't be laughing,
Two broad plates of whale-bone her body does press,
Laced up at the middle as tight as a fiddle;
With a tall, high crowned cap, it's the pride of her dress.
Her elegant form would charm any lover,
Her breath has the scent of a soap boiler's pan.
Bright Venus the charmer she may go a-wooing,
But never to death will she get a young man.

She's scarcely five feet by a couple of inches,
There's no barrel or churn her body would hold.
Her legs are like milestones, or shafts of an engine,
Her beautiful skin it's the colour of gold.
Her eyes like two diamonds, they shine like the fire,
You'd think every minute her eye strings would crack.
There's seven years dirt on her back, I'm no liar,
And a nose on her face like a West Indian black.

It's now to conclude and to finish my ditty,
Then any young fellow whose courage is bold,
Youse can come onto me and I'll give you Miss Kitty,
With all the whole farm and stock as I told.
For you may get one that's possessed of more beauty
And one's that more clean you might easily find;
But where is the farm and the stock and the money
That's what they're wanting at this very time.

Sure there could be another reason too. We'll say that a boy was
going with a girl for so many years and something happened to the
girl. Well she took ill or took sick or something, he took a notion
that she was going to be delicate or something and she wouldn't
be no good match for him and he died away just from her, because
he thought that she mightn't be strong enough to pull through
life with him. I have seen it in my own country too, that the girl
went with another boy and this man had been with her in conversation, and out with her maybe at dances and halls and everything else the most of four years anyway. So this time she went
with some other boy from a dance and this man, that was with
her, wasn't at it. So he had heard it and of course he got in bad
humour with the girl. When they met again they got into conversation about it but they never could make it up again no matter how

they tried. Outsiders tried to put them together again, that it was such a pity that they knowed each other so long and it was a pity they wouldn't get married, but in spite of all neither of them ever got married.

In my case my parents were dead. My father was dead for a number of years, my mother was dead round about three or four years before I got married. My wife's parents – one of them was dead. The mother was dead but the father was still living but he didn't mind anyway. There was a lot of cases they didn't allow them to take them. If the boy was poor and the girl was rich they wouldn't allow them for to get married. They'd be disagreeing about it and on the other side the girl's parents always wanted the man to have a lot of property and have a good home for the girl when she'd go in. There was a lot of disputes over marriages where the girl would be wealthy and maybe the man not wealthy, and on the other hand where the man'd be wealthy and the girl not. It would occur on either side. Well I remember in one case in my own country where the marriage day was set all right. These pair were going together for a number of years, for maybe two or three years and the boy was very wealthy. His parents had a lot of property and a couple or three farms of land and he was with this girl. Well she was a servant girl and she lived in a house very close by too. So when he took a notion of getting married his parents wouldn't agree to take a servant girl, and they had, in fact, the wedding day set and all for the wedding. So the parents upset it and wouldn't let him. So the next morning he was gone and nobody knowed where till about six or eight months after it. So then they discovered that he had went to America and took her over and he left the father and mother and the property, three or four farms of land and plenty of money, and he never returned. They had nobody left only themselves at the latter end. They had hardly one to give them a drink before they died, because the people was very angry at them for doing the like you know, for upsetting the wedding. The neighbours all was angry at them and none of them was in good humour. So it was a very lonesome thing. That was in my very early days, I wouldn't be passing about twelve or fourteen.

There was another time there was very wealthy people and they had one only daughter and they had this boy hired. He was away up from the upper end of the County Cavan and of course I think he fell in love with this girl when he was a period of time in it, six months or so. So when they come to know of it, her father and mother, *the row ris*. They'd put him out of that they said. So she was in a terrible way for fear he'd be taken away from her and the father wouldn't agree but put him out of that. So he banished the fellow from about the house altogether and he got another, went to the fair and got another boy to work. So he went away to America and a few months after that, in about twelve months after that, the girl left and took a very large sum of money. I don't know what it was that she took at that time, but it was a very large sum of money from the father and mother, and she left and landed in America with him. I heard they were living happy in America. I was only a small boy at the time but I knowed them myself.

Aye there's a lot of songs about that kind of thing happening. There's one, that 'Johnny Harte':

## Johnny Harte

There was a rich farmer's daughter lived near the town of
    Ross,
She was courted by a private soldier, whose name was Johnny
    Harte.
For six long months they courted, her parents did not know
That he was her gallant soldier boy no matter where she'd go.

Says the woman to the daughter, 'I will go distracted mad,
If you marry a private soldier dressed up in his ugly clad.
I know your fortune is too great and marry some farmer's
    son.'
'Oh! I'd rather have my soldier boy than any farmer's son.'

It was early the next morning her mother went to Ross,
To view the colonel's quarters as she marched it across.
The colonel being a noble man he then began to smile
And he quickly consented for to stop with her a while.

'I have one only daughter and she's a foolish lass,
She's courted by one of your soldiers whose name is Johnny
    Harte.
To court a private soldier, it's below my child's degree

84

And if you could send him out of Ross my blessing I'll give
  thee.'

Oh! the bugle sounded for parade, young Harte he did appear,
The colonel walked up to him all in the barrack square.
'If you court this woman's daughter and me to find it out,
I will send you on detachment till the regiment gets the rout.'

'It is hard enough,' young Harte replied, 'for the courting of
  an Irish lass.
To send me on detachment and leave my love in Ross.
I will court this woman's daughter and for me she's inclined,
I would court your honour's daughter could I but gain her
  mind.'

'Well done, well done, brave Harte,' he says, 'I like your
  courage well;
And you shall be promoted for the words you boldly tell.
I'll put epulates on your shoulders and then you'll be a match
For the foremost farmer's daughter that comes into the town
  of Ross.'

For to get these couple married the Colonel gave consent,
Her parents paid the portion down and now they are content.
Young Harte became an officer with his own dear captain's
  bride,
And he's one of the richest farmers that's around Lough
  Slaney side.

There was a lot of them songs about the same thing. Boys and
girls in love and the parents disputing about it and they had to
leave the country altogether. This thing was different from that
I'm after telling you because they returned to her father and he
was that glad to see her, she was seven years away, that he let her
and the boy into his estate. I learned this song from a fellow the
name of Jack Quigley. He was a very good singer too and had a
lot of comic songs too as well. Me and him met in Clones and we
went into Mrs Byrne's for a drink and he was singing me an odd
wee song and I'd sing him an odd one, and we wouldn't get leave
to sing. I suppose we had a couple of drinks on us, but nothing to
signify. But he said he'd come on out our road with me and he'd
sing a couple of songs for me out the road, when they wouldn't

give him leave to sing. We were in a wee snug me and him, a wee square hole, and she looked in and shook her hand. The company didn't allow singing do you see. Jack said he'd come on out the road and he'd sing.

Well your talking! There was a crowd in front of us, and behind us, listening and there was a schoolmaster here that was down from . . . I think he wasn't married at the time, she was his intended. He was teaching at Mullaghvan School, and he walked on after us the whole way. Jack would sing a song and I'd sing one. He said it was the best ever he heard in his life. Jack turned back. He lived beyond the town you know, outside Clones a bit, about a mile or so. When he turned back they waited on me and asked if I could have Jack down one night and me. Something went wrong, we didn't get down to it anyway. But he come up a couple of times to get me to go down to have a night singing. He was terrible fond of the songs. I'll sing you one of them anyway. It was Jack's favourite you know.

## The Lady Heiress and the Farmer's Son

Oh there was a lady heiress, she was courted by a farmer's son,
The farmer's son was handsome and won the lady's heart,
They were so far advanced in love that no answer could they
    part [no one could them part].

It was when her father came to know of his daughter's
    foolish mind,
Said, 'I will transport your love should I live till the spring-
    time.'
The spring-time it was coming and the war was just at hand,
And in the front of battle they placed that farmer's son.

'Twas there he received a deadly wound, a bullet pierced his
    heart,
'If they were here whom I love dear, they'd cure me of my
    smart.'

It was quickly to hospital this young man was conveyed,
Where there he got attendance from the Captain's waiting
    maid.
And as she turned around about, he viewed her every part,

Saying, 'Once,' said he, 'when a maid like you were mistress
of my heart.'

'You're very right young man,' said she, 'and your comforts
I'll enlarge,'
A thousand pounds she counted down to get her love
discharged.
From that to the Lord Lieutenant on her bended knee she
prayed,
Till she brought her love into Ireland across the raging seas.

And when she came to her father's gate she traillied for a
while,
Her da-da hid in the window, 'Here comes my darling child.'
Saying, 'Daughter dear where have you been for seven long
years or more?'
'I was seeking for my own true love he's the lad that I adore.'

He took her by the lily-white hand and he strove to bring
her in,
'Oh no my honoured father except you bring in him,
For money's good and it's very good, but love exceeds it far,
'Twas all for the sake of my own true love that I boldly faced
the war.'

Aye this man sung a lot and had a lot of old songs. Of course
he was an aged man when I used to be ceilidhing in it at night.
He'd be seventy-six or seven. He would be dead I suppose thirty-
five or thirty-six years ago. He had been living *his lone* for a
number of years, the wife had died ten or twelve years before that.
So I thought it very amusing to go on the ceilidh nights to hear
him. He was a real good comic singer. That's how I learned that
song. Most of his songs were comic songs. I'm sure there's some
of them I have related over the country for the last forty or fifty
years. Some of them was very good now. There was 'The Tailor
from Tyrone', did I not give you that one?

## The Wee Tailor from Tyrone

Oh I am a little tailor, I was born in Tyrone,
I courted lovely Mollie till I thought I had her won.

She vowed for I to marry her, to that I'd ne'er agree,
And ready to get shot of her I'd rather till or deal.

CHORUS
Ladily fall all te laady, fall all te lee,
Ladily fall all te laady, wasn't she able enough for me.

Oh I was not long now at my work, past one day, two or
   three,
Till my rousing little Mollie she got there as well as me.
She ne'er showed her appearance, when she heard I were at
   trade,
But she hired with a lady for to be her waiting maid.

CHORUS

She wrote to me a letter, she lived lonely in the town,
And if I'd agree to marry her I'd be worth ten thousand
   pound.
Oh when I read the letter, sure my heart it jumped with joy,
Saying it's better be a gentleman, than live apprentice boy.

CHORUS

When I went until the lady's house she took me by the hand,
She kindily saluted me, 'Come in you gentleman.
I hope you will be seated, if you be my noble spark,
For if you and I gets married sure it must be in the dark.'

CHORUS

'Now the Priest he will not marry us because we are too
   young,
And when the words are saying you must alter your tongue.'
The Priest that came to marry us had neither hat nor cloak,
The lady she stepped forward and she told him of the joke.

CHORUS

Aha now when that we were married and the nut was tied so
   tight,
Then I asked it of the lady for to grant to me some light.
'I hope you will excuse me if you know what's in my head,
There will be no light drawn till dawn, till we're left safe in
   bed.'

CHORUS

Oh then I took off my small clothes for to get in bed in
  peace,
I content, you may be sure when I couldn't see her face.
I turned to embrace her, I knew my love at once,
'Is this my rousing Mollie, in soul it is by chance.'

'Ah but you thought you were a gentleman, and now you see
  you're none,
Ach you're a naughty little tailor, you were begging through
  Tyrone.'

CHORUS


There's another song:


## Marrow Bones

There was a pretty lady near to Carlow town did dwell,
She loved her own man dearly and another one twice as well.

CHORUS
Til my rigidy orum-dorum and it's rigidy oram day
Rigidy oram-doram, Och! and it's right fall turra lay.

Oh she went until the Doctor's shop to see if she could find
Some kind of medicine for to set this old man blind.

CHORUS

Ah she brought for him nine marrow bones she gave them to
  him all,
Before he had the last one sucked he couldn't see her at all.

CHORUS

'Oh it's Biddy I am getting blind, at home I cannot stay,
Sure I would go and drownd myself, if I could see my way.'

CHORUS

'Oh John you are blind and at home you cannot stay,
But if you wish to drownd yourself I'll show you the right
  way.'

CHORUS

89

Oh they walked along and they talked along, to they came to
the river brim,
He says, 'My dear and beloved wife you will shove me in.'

CHORUS

Oh then she stepped a few yards back, came with all her skill;
Cunning enough he stepped one side and she went tumbling
in.

CHORUS

When she was a-drownding on mercy she did call.
He says, 'My dear and beloved wife I can't see you at all.'

CHORUS

Now this old man he was tender-hearted he knew she could
not swim;
With a big long pole he brought from home he puddled her
further in.

CHORUS

Now this old man he has seven kids there's none of them his
own.
He's wishing for every decent man to come and take he's own.

CHORUS

In my days if a man and wife couldn't get on too well together
the man generally always left and went to some other country.
I knowed a case in my own country where a couple of men left
and one went to Scotland and another went to England and they
never returned in my time. I remember before that an old fellow
used to tell me about if they disagreed when they were married
well the law was, at that time, the man could auction the wife.
He was the name of Patrick Caddin beside me. I have a comic
song of he's about it:

## In Praise of John Magee

It's in praise of John Magee who had auctioned out his wife,
She was such a damned old villain, she had plagued him all
his life,

Ah! no ease nor contentment with her he could find;
How to get rid of her came into his mind.

CHORUS
Diddly-di-addle-dum, diddly-doodle-eedle-dum,
Di-ad-a doodle diddly-dum diddly-da.
Tar-ri-ar-a-ri-iddly-diddly-dump,
Diddly-di-a-da-diddle-e-e-dum-diddly-da.

When the chimley-sweeper's wife heard the auctioneer roar,
With a stone in her stocking she gave him a blow
He up with his crutch and he knocked this woman down
The sweep with the broom, came crack upon her crown.

CHORUS

The first that came up was a jolly roving tar,
And he on his way from the Indian war.
He waited till he heard the auctioneer roar
No matter what the bidding would be he'd bid a shilling more.

CHORUS

Oh a jobber from Killarney for the auction he did wait,
With his mouth wide open like a Newton-gate.
Oh! he took a look upon and he said that she would do
'She's a damn nice figure and well rigged too.'

CHORUS

Well the next that came up was a farmer riding by,
He bought this old woman aye at shillings twenty-five.
Now he being a widow and a friend of her own,
He stuck her up behind him and they both drove home.

CHORUS

It's now for to finish and end all my strife,
John Magee has got home but he hasn't got a wife.
'Well the devil run along with him,' the auctioneer did say;
And 'Amen', said the women, 'sure we'll all buy away.'

CHORUS

Well this time that I got married there wasn't as big parties at
weddings as there is today. You could get sixty or seventy or a

hundred at a wedding, but there was only about ten or twelve at our wedding altogether. Just the bridesmaid and best-man and another few neighbours about. So when you got married at that time you went away on your honeymoon in the afternoon and we went to Bundoran. We stayed there for about ten days. I think it was the Royal Hotel there, it was at that time. For the ten days that we were in it it cost us about seven pound. My brother Brian was there at home you know, he was best-man, he looked after the farm. When we came back we moved into the house over there in Tonaydrumallard.

The house was a thatched house and the thatch was gone very badly on it and I had to start to repair. So I started and got a few carpenters and workmen and expanded out the house, a couple of blocks higher, and put a roof on it, corrugated iron. So then I had outhouses, when I had that done, for to put up. There was a stand of a barn but we had to roof it with iron. I got that all done within a few years, we'll say about two or three years. So still I was making improvements until a couple of years ago, to I retired myself, and give it to my son John Joe. Well the farm part of it wasn't in good condition and other parts of it was. There were six or eight fields of it in fair good condition but there was other parts of it, up at the marsh, wasn't. With another man, Cosgrove, I had to drain it and clean *the shores* on it, cut the rushes off it, and it took a couple of years for to leave it fertile, that it would give either grass or crop. I had to work very long hours, probably many's the morning I was up at six o'clock in the morning and I might be working till about nine or ten that night and I got a young fellow for to help me three days a week. At that time they used to consent to come to you half-time, three days in the week. So I got him to help me cleaning up the land and clearing the shores round it and doing the work about the place, helping me to milk and feed pigs and help the wife for to do the trips about the house. Sometimes she done the milking all, and this boy that come would help her some evenings and so on. She always reared turkeys. She reared a lot of fowl and done the work of the house. Several times, if it was needed, she come to the field and helped us to work in the field as well.

You have a lot of worries on a farm too. You must look, as the old fellow said, a year or two years in front of you. In the first place I had to stock the land. I had to buy four or five cows, a

couple or three heifers and some calves, some pigs to fatten. I
had to put that all on the place at the time. Well as a run the
cattle wasn't that dear at that time, it's different from now. A
cow would only cost about fourteen pounds. You bought a good
cow for it and you bought a good calf for seven or eight pound.
So you bought a sucking pig for about thirty shillings, so that
left things not so bad. At that time there was a lot of corn and
potatoes put in and it took all the help you could get to get through
four or five acres of corn and a couple of acres of spuds. At that
time there was subsidies on crop. There was ten pound an acre
on potatoes and four or five pound of subsidy on corn. You put
in as much of it as you could.

There was, for the first one or two years, I was still spending
money. I wasn't getting very much because I had too much to
do and I was getting very little money, but the first thing I started
was to go to the fairs and markets and buy the odd springing heifer
or two maybe three, and some *stirks* and turn them over. And
that was the first money I could say I received in profit. From
thirty-eight or forty I went more into stock. The subsidy had
flowed by by that time. I used to go out and deal in springing
heifers, bring them home and calve them and sell the cow and
calf. So you could nearly always gauge it to have the price of the
calf out of the cow. It was worth *a fiver* as a rule. I still kept some
crop on but I didn't do as much at it. Once there was no subsidy
on them they wouldn't pay to put in too much.

There's a terrible big change now. The farming in my early days
it was done with a spade and shovel and hook for cutting corn and
the scythe. Well it has changed now to tractors doing all them
works. Machines on them for cutting hay what used to be cut with
a scythe. The horses done a lot of work with the machine too, they
cut the whole hay and all for a good many years. I used to be joined
with an old fellow they called John the Captain. He lived over the
river from us. My son Hughie has the place now. Always at that
time we'd have horses apiece. He had a horse and I had a horse
and as a rule in this country two men like that always joined in
ploughing and putting in the crop. You only had the one horse to
feed and the farms wasn't that big and two horses could do the
both farms. You needed two horses to plough and two horses to
break harrow or put in drills, everything. You needed both horses
for it. So they always joined, neighbours that would be beside

other, it was the handiest way. He'd put in six or seven acres and I'd put in the same and we worked that way.

The last of the horses was I suppose it's ten or fifteen years ago. There was odd people had horses later on than that now but they were in the country for twenty-five or thirty years. Then they moved into the tractors. There was parts of the country the horses, I suppose, was the best for it. If it wasn't ground to suit them, the tractors was bad. If it was damp ground or anything like the tractors didn't do any good on it. You'd have a better crop ploughing or harrowing with horses. I suppose like everything else, like the young fellows driving the motor-car, they weren't quick enough. They wanted the job quicker done. There's not as hard work now at all only there's more of it to be done. It's more, as the old man said, mass production now. You have a lot more of it to go through than you did at that time. There's a lot of them moving away out of it, which that's leaving farms far bigger for one man to handle. Some of the farms mightn't be so much bigger but they have three or four times the stock. Maybe some of them nine or ten times the stock they had at that time, of cattle and pigs and sows and everything. He needs a quicker way of doing it now.

We have three of a family. Hughie was the oldest, he'd be thirty-one and Bridie that's married to Tommy Beggen, she's about thirty and John Joe would be twenty-seven. That's the family. Was according to they got up, Hughie went to school about six year old. Him and Bridie went together. She was only four and a half and John Joe was about four and a half when he went to school too. Well they had to stay at school at them times till they'd be fourteen. Then in the latter end they had to stay till they were fifteen. So they got a fair education. Bridie was married first. She's ten years married and she has seven of a family, six boys and a wee girl. Hughie was married about three years after that and he has four of a family, two wee boys and two wee girls. John Joe's married about three years now. He has a wee baby girl, she's twelve months old now.

The boys never wrought away much, they wrought on the farm mostly. They were a good help. From ever they got up they were a good help. Hughie used to work with a horse and cart, he drew turf and he drew manure out for potatoes. So did John Joe too. They were a big help. Then Hughie was living on that man's place, 'the Captain's'. We have got that place and he was living

94

on it since he got married – seven years or thereaways. And there last year he bought another place, the name of Hughie Boyle owned it, because it was closer to the road than that. Now he works both places. I have retired now. I give them that farm of 'the Captain's' and he bought the one that he has. John Joe's on the farm that me and her started on first. He's still working away on it yet. Of course he has a good deal of places, as well, taken and he has a very big stock of both sows and pigs and cattle and everything.

I decided to retire when I was sixty-five. I didn't think there was any call me working any longer, holding the reins any longer from the childer, and the pension helps too. Then when John Gallagher was going away out of his place John Joe was married over there in Tonaydrumallard. So we thought we'd have more comfort here, not be all living in the one house, we moved over. John asked me would we come to this place.* So it was very handy and it was very handy for John Joe as well, for the stock that he had about it. I could still be a wee bit help to him and I was better doing a wee little.

The future is I suppose take as good a time as I can. Not but I'm still working, working away as hard nearly sometimes as ever. It's not always now, I just take a better time nor I did. I go oftener to the towns, do you know, nor I used to go. More time. It's like what the old fellow said, 'It's come day, go day, God send Sunday!'

* Knocknagross, the townland next to Tonaydrumallard.

# A note on the musical transcription

## *John Blacking*

All transcriptions were taken direct from original recordings of John Maguire's performances taken by Robin Morton. In many cases, more than one performance was available for study; and in all songs, the variations in melody for different verses were noted. In the present study only the first verse, together with an occasional common variation, is given for each song. An analytical study of the songs and John Maguire's style will be published later.

The transcriptions represent as accurately as possible how John Maguire sang to the words given, and no attempt has been made to force his performances into an idealized metrical framework, or to pick out the basic melodic pattern which is followed in all verses. The recordings were transcribed by listening many times to each phrase, sometimes at half speed, and checking the rhythms against regular beats. After an interval of some months, most recordings were studied again, and then again, so as to ensure the utmost accuracy in the absence of an electronic device such as a melograph. In spite of this, the transcriptions can be only an approximate representation of John Maguire's style and the individuality of his tone of voice.

The long-playing record of some of his performances will convey more than all the transcriptions; but those who wish to sing the songs for themselves should note that in all songs except those that are marked 'in strict time' (and sometimes even in these), the rhythm and content of the words are crucial influences on performance. Also the last phrase of most of the songs was spoken, almost like a stage aside and without rhythmic emphasis. This is a common practice among traditional singers in these islands and seems to be used to signify the end of the song.

No time-signatures are given, and pauses between each line of verse are indicated as accurately as possible by the note value of the last tone in each line, and by the insertion of rests wherever there is a pause longer than that generally required for breath. The basic pulse and rhythm of song is implied by the note value chosen for the metronome markings, and bar-lines indicate the general pattern of accentuation. Where the rhythm is very free and 'word-bound', half-bar-lines are used. The songs in fairly strict time are those which are so marked.

Slurs are included only to indicate where more than one tone accompanies a single syllable of the words. In a very few cases, common alternative tones are given with their tails pointing in the opposite direction. A distinction has been made between grace-notes which are 'squeezed into' a melody and those which seem to be an integral part of John Maguire's singing style. The former are given as acciaccaturas, but the latter are written as basic melody. This may seem to be an unwarranted, arbitrary distinction which does not truly represent what is in the mind of the singer. There can be no defence for this practice except that it aims to reproduce differences which are clearly audible in the recordings.

# Music for songs in the text

## 1. Molly Bawn Lowry

Transposed down a semitone

Come all you late fow-lers that car-ry a gun,
Be-ware of late fowl-ing in the dark of the sun;
Be-ware of late fowl-ing, when what hap-pened of late,
It was Mol-ly Bawn Low-ry and a-hard was her fate.

## 2. Columbia the Free

Co-lum-bia the free, it's the land of my birth;
My pack is all o-ver A-mer-i-can earth.
My blood is as I-rish as I-rish can be,
And me heart's in green E-rin far o-ver the sea.

99

## 3. Willie's Ghost

Transposed up a semitone

$\flat = 72$

Oh Wil - lie dear where are the blush - es

That you had some time a - go?

Oh Ma - ry dear the cold clay changed them,

For I'm the ghost of your Wil - lie O.

That night they spent in deep dis - cours - ing

Of the court - ships they had some time a - go.

They kissed, shook hands, with a sor - row - ful part - ing

As the cocks they be-gan to crow.

## 4. Behind Yon Blue Mountain

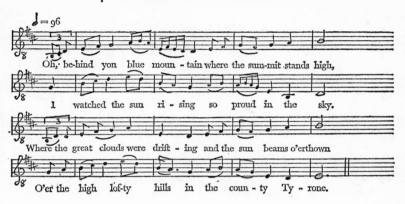

Oh, be-hind yon blue moun - tain where the sum-mit stands high,

I watched the sun ri - sing so proud in the sky.

Where the great clouds were drift - ing and the sun beams o'erthown

O'er the high lof-ty hills in the coun - ty Ty - rone.

## 5. Lovely Jane from Enniskea

One eve - ning fair in love - ly June I care - less - ly did stray,

The fields with ac - clam - a - tion rang, and flow - ers decked each vale,

Fair and de - light - ful was the scene, and one thing seemed more gay,

And that was Jane that's free from stain in love - ly En-nis - kea.

## 6. The Maid of Magheracloon

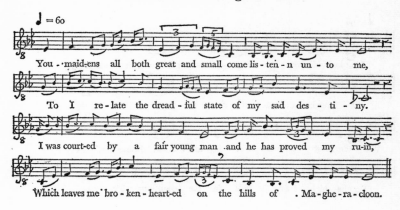

You maidens all both great and small come listen unto me,
To I relate the dreadful state of my sad destiny.
I was courted by a fair young man and he has proved my ruin,
Which leaves me broken-hearted on the hills of Magheracloon.

## 7. The Pony Song

Let the pony go fast as e'er it will,
Dobbin sure you know when he reached a hill.
What a merry ride, how we jog along,
See how snugly side by side and joining in a song.
Jinkle bells, jinkle bells, jinkle all the way,
Oh the funny ride we had down by Ennis-kea.

## 8. Tom Kelly's Cow

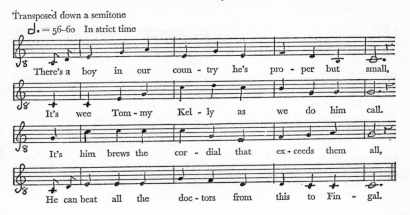

Transposed down a semitone

♩. = 56–60   In strict time

There's a boy in our coun - try he's pro - per but small,

It's wee Tom - my Kel - ly as we do him call.

It's him brews the cor - dial that ex - ceeds them all,

He can beat all the doc - tors from this to Fin - gal.

## 9. The Molly Maguires

Transposed down a semitone

♩. = 63

Oh it's in the praise of Mol - ly's sons I'm go - ing to sing a song;

They are a no - ble bo - dy, to her they do be - long.

They are a no - ble bo - dy and they're stur - dy, stout and free;

They can root out all De - fen - ders and plant the Lau - rel Tree.

## 10. Hunting Song

There's a-no-ther fine dog they call Ti - mer,
He's ·yet the best hound e - ver run.
For when that the hare sees him com - ing,
She knows that her life's near - ly run.

## 11. The Follom Brown-Red

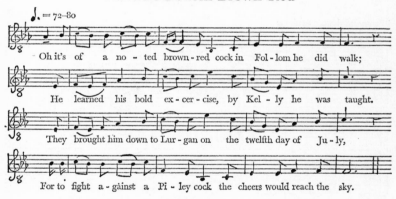

Oh it's of a no - ted brown-red cock in Fol-lom he did walk;
He learned his bold ex-cer-cise, by Kel-ly he was taught.
They brought him down to Lur-gan on the twelfth day of Ju-ly,
For to fight a-gainst a Pi-ley cock the cheers would reach the sky.

## 12. Sergeant Neill

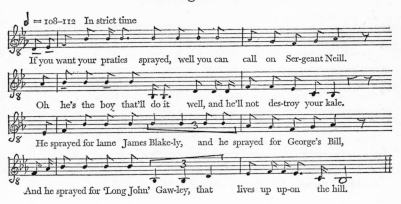

♩ = 108–112 In strict time

If you want your praties sprayed, well you can call on Ser-geant Neill.

Oh he's the boy that'll do it well, and he'll not des-troy your kale.

He sprayed for lame James Blake-ly, and he sprayed for George's Bill,

And he sprayed for 'Long John' Gaw-ley, that lives up up-on the hill.

## 13. John Barleygrain

Transposed up a semitone·

♩ = 96 . In strict time

Oh John Bar-ley is the rar - est grain,

That e'er you sowed on land.

It far ex - ceeds than a - ny o - ther grain

With the cast that you give your hand.

Ah to the le-gum - ba - - tar-ry oo - dle ah

John Bar - ley - grain's for me.

## 14. The Strabane Hiring Fair

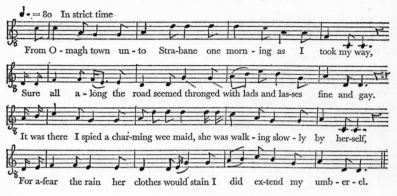

♩. = 80  In strict time

From O - magh town un - to Stra-bane one morn - ing as I took my way,

Sure all a - long the road seemed thronged with lads and las-ses fine and gay.

It was there I spied a char-ming wee maid, she was walk - ing slow - ly by her-self,

For a-fear the rain her clothes would stain I did ex-tend my umb - er - el.

## 15. Thousands Are Sailing to America

Transposed down a semitone

Oh you brave I - rish peo - ple, wher - e - ver you be,

I pray stand a mo - ment and lis - ten to me.

Your sons and brave daugh - ters are now going a - way,

And thou - sands are sail - ing to A - mer - i - key.

Ah good luck to them now, and safe may they land,

They are push - ing their way to a far dis - tant strand,

For here in old Ire - land no long - er can stay,

For thou - sands are sail - ing to A - mer - i - key.

## 16. Fee and Flannigan

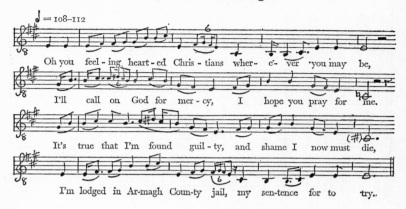

Oh you feel - ing heart - ed Chris - tians wher- e'- ver 'you may be,

I'll call on God for mer - cy, I hope you pray for me.

It's true that I'm found guil - ty, and shame I now must die,

I'm lodged in Ar-magh Coun-ty jail, my sen-tence for to try.

## 17. The Constant Farmer's Son

There was a rich far - mer's daugh-ter near Li-me-rick town did dwell;

She was mo-dest fair and hand - some, her par - ents loved her well.

She was ad - mired by lords and squires, but all their hopes in vain;

There was but one young far - mer's son now Ma - ry's heart did gain. .

## 18. Young Mary from Kilmore

Transposed up a semitone

You gods of love I pray draw near and lend to me some aid;

It's here I am en-deav-our-ing to praise a char-min' maid.

She's pro-per, tall and hand-some, has a-woun-ded my heart sore,

Oh she is the bloom-ing fair one, young Ma-ry from Kil-more.

## 19. My Charming Mary

Fare - well dear E - rin, I now must leave you
And cross the seas to a for-eign clime.
Fare - well to friends and kind re - la - tions,.
And 'til my par - ents I left be-hind.
Fare - well green hills, and your sweet love - ly val - leys,
Where with my love I did oft - times roam,
And fond - ly told her I ne'er would leave her,
While walk - ing in yon si - lent grove.

## 20. Joe Higgins

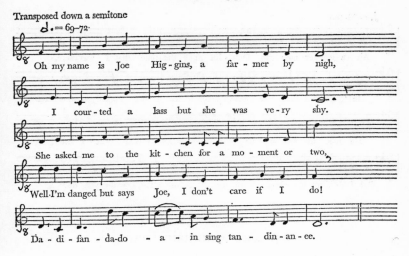

Transposed down a semitone

♩. = 69–72.

Oh my name is Joe Hig-gins, a far-mer by nigh,

I cour-ted a lass but she was ve-ry shy.

She asked me to the kit-chen for a mo-ment or two,

Well·I'm danged but says Joe, I don't care if I do!

Da - di - fan - da-do - a - in sing tan - din-an-ee.

## 21. Bold Jack Donohue

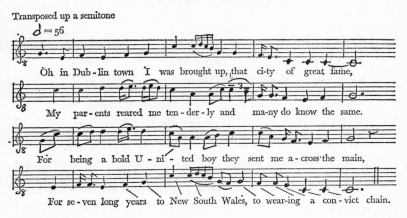

Transposed up a semitone

♩ = 56

Oh in Dub-lin town I was brought up, that ci-ty of great fame,

My par-ents reared me ten-der-ly and ma-ny do know the same.

For being a bold U - ni - ted boy they sent me a-cross·the main,

For se-ven long years to New South Wales, to wear-ing a con-vict chain.

## 22. The Gauger's Song

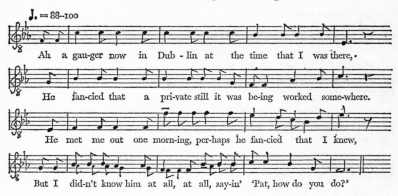

Ah a gau-ger now in Dub - lin at the time that I was there,

He fan-cied that a pri-vate still it was be-ing worked some-where.

He met me out one morn-ing, per-haps he fan-cied that I knew,

But I did-n't know him at all, at all, say-in' 'Pat, how do you do?'

## 23. The Mountain Dew

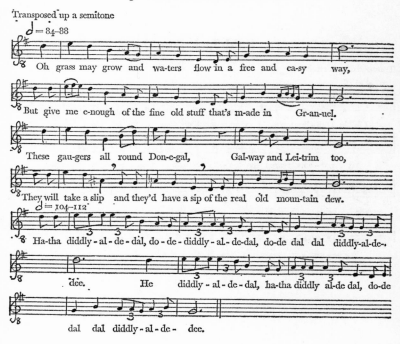

Oh grass may grow and wa-ters flow in a free and ea-sy way,

But give me e-nough of the fine old stuff that's m-ade in Gr-an-uel.

These gau-gers all round Don-e-gal, Gal-way and Lei-trim too,

They will take a slip and they'd have a sip of the real old moun-tain dew.

Ha-tha diddly - al - de - dal, do - de - diddly - al - de-dal, do-de dal dal diddly-al-de-.

dee. He diddly - al - de-dal, ha-tha diddly al-de dal, do-de

dal dal diddly - al - de - dee.

## 24. Lough Ooney

Oh you bards of this na - tion, and sons of old E - 'rin.

Come join me in deep con - sol - a - tion,

'Since a he - ro of fame, no - ble Mur-ray by name,

And a friend 'til our great I - rish na - tion.

Your gods to in - voke all their sweets to en - joy,

His spouse was far fair - er nor Ju - - - no.

For the plains of Co - lum - ba could ne - ver com - pare,

'Til the love - ly sweet shades of Lough Oo - ney.

## 25. The Handsome Collier Lad

My love he is a col-li-er lad, he works all un-der-ground,

His mod-est mild be-ha-viour is no-where can be found;

His dark blue eyes, his cur-ly hair, and cheeks of ro-sy red,

But a-las my hand-some col-li-er lad, he's n-um-bered with the dead.

## 26. The Maid of the Colehill

It being on the se-venth of Jan-u-a-ry

When go'ng to the 'Bridge Fair,

I met a bon-nie las-sie,

Combed down her yel-low hair.

The a-more that I did gaze on her

My heart with love did fill,

She's my beau-ty's bright, my heart's de-light,

She's the maid of the Cole-hill.

## 27. The Blantyre Explosion

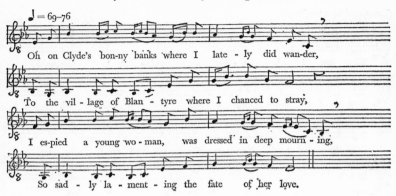

♩ = 69–76

Oh on Clyde's bon-ny banks where I late - ly did wan-der,

To the vil - lage of Blan - tyre where I chanced to stray,

I es-pied a young wo-man, was dressed in deep mourn - ing,

So sad - ly la - ment - ing the fate of her love.

## 28. Blooming Caroline from Edinburgh Town

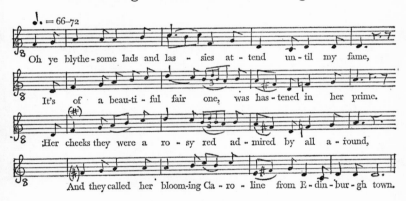

♩. = 66–72

Oh ye blythe - some lads and las - sies at - tend un - til my fame,

It's of a beau-ti - ful fair one, was has - tened in her prime.

Her cheeks they were a ro - sy red ad - mired by all a - round,

And they called her bloom-ing Ca - ro - line from E - din - bur-gh town.

## 29. The Glasgow Barber

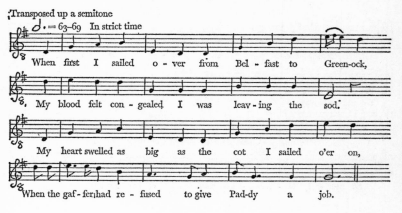

Transposed up a semitone

♩. = 63–69  In strict time

When first I sailed o - ver from Bel - fast to Green-ock,

My blood felt con - gealed. I was leav - ing the sod.

My heart swelled as big as the cot I sailed o'er on,

When the gaf - fer had re - fused to give Pad-dy a job.

## 30. The Bonnie Wee Lassie that Never Said No

♩. = 69-72

Oh you folks of this na - tion of high and low sta - tion,

All you wee las - ses give ear to my song.

If you lis - ten a while it'll cause you to smile;

It's not my in - ten - tion to keep you too long.

At a cross-roads as I passed sure I met a wee lass,

And I asked her if she'd be quite wil - ling to go,

Take share in a gill, she says 'Yes sir, I will!'

For I'm the wee las - sie' that ne-ver said no!'

## 31. Dick Mooney's Daughter

Transposed down a semitone

My name is Dick Moo-ney, I'm now just a - dy - ing,

I have but one daugh-ter is want-ing a man.

It is my in - ten - tion her for - tune to men - tion,

To get her a hus-band as soon as I can.

A house and a gar-den, a snug lit - tle farm,

Three cows that are tied that her grand - mo - ther sent,

And an old breed-ing mare, she's blind I de-clare,

She'll be thir - ty years old at the first of next Lent.

## 32. Johnny Harte

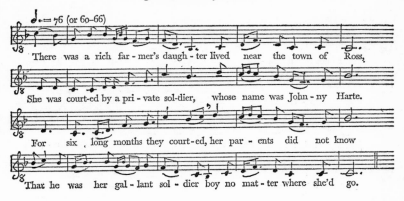

There was a rich far-mer's daugh-ter lived near the town of Ross,

She was court-ed by a pri-vate sol-dier, whose name was John-ny Harte.

For six long months they court-ed, her par-ents did not know

That he was her gal-lant sol-dier boy no mat-ter where she'd go.

## 33. The Lady Heiress and the Farmer's Son

Oh there was a la-dy heir-ess, she was court-ed by a far-mer's son,

The far-mer's son was hand-some and won the la-dy's heart,

They were so far ad-vanced in love that no an-swer could they part.

It was when her fa-ther came to know of his daugh-ter's fool-ish mind,

Said "I will trans-port your love should I live till the spring-time.

The spring-time it was com-ing and the war was just at hand,

And in the front of bat-tle they placed that far-mer's son.

## 34. The Wee Tailor from Tyrone

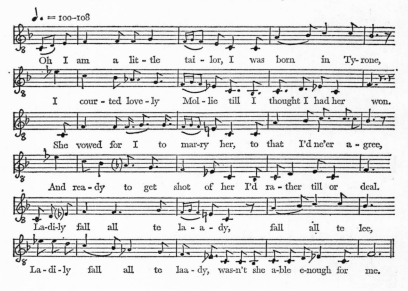

Oh I am a lit - tle tai - lor, I was born in Ty- rone,

I cour - ted love - ly Mol - lie till I thought I had her won.

She vowed for I to mar - ry her, to that I'd ne'er a - gree,

And rea - dy to get shot of her I'd ra - ther till or deal.

La-di-ly fall all te la - a - dy, fall all te lee,

La - di - ly fall all te laa - dy, was - n't she a-ble e-nough for me.

## 35. Marrow Bones

♩. = 100–108

There was a pret-ty la-dy near to Car-low town did dwell,

She loved her own man dear-'ly and a-no-ther one twice as well.

Slightly faster

Til my ri-gi-dy o-rum do-rum and it's ri-gi-dy o-rum day,

Ri-gi-dy o-ram do-ram, Och! and it's right-fall tur-ra-lay.

Oh she went un-til the Doc-tor's shop to see if she could find

Some kind of me-di-cine for to set this old man blind.

## 36. In Praise of John Magee

It's in praise of John Ma-gee who had auc - tioned out his wife,

She was such a damned old vil - lain, she had plagued him all his life.

Ah! no ease nor con - tent - ment with her he could find;

How to get rid of her came in - to his mind.

Diddly - di - addle - dum, diddly - doodle - eedle - dum

Di - ad - a doodle diddly - dum diddly - da;

Tar - - ri - ar - a - ri - iddly - diddly - dump,

Diddly - di - a - da - diddle - e - a - dum - diddly - da.

# Further songs with music

## 37. The Old Leather Britches

Transposed down a semitone

At the sign of the Bell on the road to Clon-mel,

Pat Ha - ger - ty kept a fine ca-bin.

He sold whis - key and bread, he kept lod - gers be - sides;

He was liked in the coun - try he lived in.

Po - or Pat and his wife, they strug - gled through life;

On week-days he men-ded the dit - ches;

On Sun-day he dressed in a coat of the best,

But his pride was them old leath - er brit - ches.

At the sign of the Bell on the road to Clonmel,
Pat Hagerty kept a fine cabin,
He sold whiskey and bread, he kept lodgers besides;
He was liked in the country he lived in.
Poor Pat and his wife, they struggled through life
On weekdays he mended the ditches;
On Sunday he dressed in a coat of the best,
But his pride was them old leather britches.

For twenty-one years, at least so it appears,
Pat's father these britches he run in.
The morning he died all to his bedside
He called Paddy his own darling son in.
Advice then he gave ere he went to his grave,
For he couldn't boast of his riches.
He says 'It's no use to get into my shoes,
But I'd like you'd step into the britches.'

Oh then last winter's snow brought vittels so low
That poor Paddy was ate out completely.
The snow coming down, he could not get to town,
And hunger it bothered him greatly.
One night as he lay a-dreaming away,
About ghosts, fairies, spirits and witches,
He heard an uproar just outside of the door
And he jumped up to pull on the britches.

Says Barry McGurk with a voice like a Turk,
'Now Paddy get us some eating.'
Says Big Andy Moore, 'We'll break in the door,
For this is no night to be waiting.'
The word was scarce spoke when the door it was broke
And they crowded round Paddy like leeches.
They swore by the mob if they didn't get grub,
That they'd eat him clean out of his britches.

Ah poor Paddy in dread slipped up to bed
And held Judy his own darling wife in,
And there it was agreed that they should get the feed,
So he slipped out and brought a big knife in
He cut off the waist of his britches;
He ripped out the buttons and stiches.

He cut them in stripes in the way they'd make tripes,
And boiled them, his old leather britches.

Oh the tripes they stewed, on the dishes were strewed,
The boys they roared out, God be thankéd;
But Hagerty's wife got afraid of her life,
And she thought it high time for to shank it.
To see how they smiled, they thought Paddy had boiled
Some mutton or beef of the richest;
But little they knew it was leather brogúe,
That was made out of Paddy's old britches.

As they looked on the stuff says Darby, 'It's tough';
And says Andy, 'You're no judge of mutton'.
When Brian McGurk on the point of his fork,
He held up a big pair of buttons.
Says Paddy, 'What's that? Sure I thought it was fat';
Brian jumps up and he screeches,
'By the powers above I was trying to shove
All my teeth through the flap of his britches.'

They all flew at Pat, but he cut out of that
When he saw them all rising.
Says Brian 'Make haste and go for the priest,
For by Holy Saint Patrick I'm poisoned.'
Revenge for the joke for they had all broke,
All the chairs, tables, bottles and dishes.
From that very night they'd knock out your delight,
If you mentioned old leather britches.

## 38. The Gay Ploughboy

Transposed down a semitone

♩ = 104

There was a rich far-mer's daugh-ter in this north coun-ter-y,
.She had sweet-hearts now plen-ty of ever-y de-gree.
She 'roved in great splen-dour, and free from all care,
To her fa-ther's gay plough-boy did her whole heart en-snare.

There was rich farmer's daughter in this north country,
She had sweethearts now plenty of every degree.
She roved in great splendour, and free from all care,
To her father's gay ploughboy did her whole heart ensnare.

One day as she drove round her father's demesne,
This gallant gay ploughboy he was ploughing the plains.
He whistled so melodiously and he sang a fine song,
For to cheer up his horses as they plough-jogged along.
He whistled so melodiously, caused the valleys to sound;
And the birds in their branches kept silent all round.

She called on her ploughboy for to hold for a while;
He turned around, with a laugh and a smile.
Her cheeks blushed like roses and thus she did say,
'You have won me completely, all alone where I stray.'

'If your father was listening 'til our discourse;
He'd punish you severely and take no excuse;
But I will take from him it's twelve hundred pounds,
And you'll be no more a ploughboy, or a tiller of ground.'

It was early next morning that the fair maid arose
Twelve hundred bright guineas to her ploughboy she throws;
'No more we are left for to plough or to sow,
You're a gallant gay ploughboy and abroad we must go.'

126

From Belfast next morning these couple set sail,
I wish them safely landed, with a free pleasant gale.
I wish them safely landed, across the salt sea,
And she's blessed by her ploughboy in the North Amerikey.

## 39. The Dandy Apprentice Boy

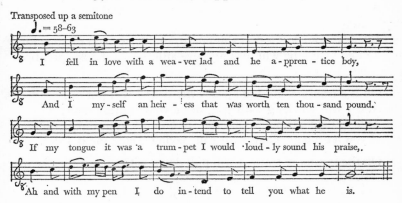

Transposed up a semitone

I fell in love with a weaver lad and he apprentice boy,
And I myself an heiress that was worth ten thousand pound.
If my tongue it was a trumpet I would loudly sound his praise,
Ah and with my pen I do intend to tell you what he is.

Oh my love he is one of the nicest men that ever your eye did
see;
His cheeks they are a rosy red and his teeth like ivory;
His skin's as white as any snow, that e'er on earth did fall
Ah go where he will he's my love still, he's a dandy 'prentice
boy.

As me and my love in the garden stood, all under a willow
tree,
Embracing one and other as I used her tenderly
We both sat down upon the ground for to condole [converse]
our joy,
Ah go where he will he's my love still, he's a dandy 'prentice
boy.

Ah, the waiting maid in the garden stood to listen what we
  would say,
And ran and told her dada without any more delay;
'Your daughter's making plots of love with your apprentice
  boy,

And she will disgrace your family, her mind to satisfy.'
It was when her dada heard it, he in a passion flew.
Saying, 'I'll use you most severely and I'll send your love
  away;
I'll send your love upon shipboard, to deprive you of your joy.'
'Oh go where he will he's my love still, he's a dandy 'prentice
  boy.'

Oh it's trousers and blue jersey my dear I will put on,
And I will go along with you, to be your waiting man;
And whilst your hours that they're on deck your duty I will do,
If you let me go along with you, saying 'Dang me if I do'.

Oh the sycamore leaves I will pull down with them I'll make my
  bed;
The laurel and the ivy I will plant it at my head.
No junifer-rue will me subdue, nor no man will me enjoy,
And so she sang and the valleys rang and she gained her
  apprentice boy.

## 40. The Bonny Irish Boy

♩ = 56

Oh when first that I was court-ed by a bon-ny I - rish boy,

He cal - led me his jew - el, his heart's de - light and joy..

It were in Dub - lin ci - ty the place of no - ted fame,

Where first my bon-ny I - rish boy a - court-ing me he came.

Oh when first that I was courted by a bonny Irish boy,
He called me his jewel, his heart's delight and joy.
It were in Dublin city the place of noted fame,
Where first my bonny Irish boy a-courting me he came.

Oh his cheeks they were a rosy red, his hair was a light brown.
His locks were curled in ringlets, o'er his shoulders hanging
    down.
His teeth were an ivory white and his eyes as black as sloes,
He breaks the heart of all the girls no matter where he goes.

Long time I kept his company in hopes to be his bride,
But now he's gone and left me to cross the raging tide.
I fear some other fair one my true love will enjoy,
Whilst I am left lamenting for my bonny Irish boy.

Oh but I'll pack up my clothing, in search of him I'll go.
I'll wander for my true love through rain, frost and snow;
And when that I am wearied, sure I can sit down and cry,
And just think upon the joys I had with my bonny Irish boy.

Oh when that I am dead and gone there's one request I'll
    crave,
To bring my bones to Ireland and leave them in my grave.
These words write on my tombstone, to tell the passers-by
That I died quite broken hearted for my bonny Irish boy.

## 41. The Factory Girl

As I went a-walking on a fine summer's morning,
The birds in yon bushes so sweetly did sing.
Gay lads and gay lasses together were sporting,
Going down 'til yon factory their work 'til begin.

As I went a-walking on a fine summer's morning,
The birds in yon bushes so sweetly did sing.
Gay lads and gay lasses together were sporting,
Going down 'til yon factory their work 'til begin.

I espied a wee lass, she was fairer nor Venus,
With cheeks like the red rose, none can her excel;
Her skin like the lily that bloomed in yon valley,
She's the one only god of sweet factory girls.

I stepped it up to her, it was for to view her,
And on me she cast a proud look of distain.
'Stand off me, stand off me young man,' she made answer,
'For the more I'm poor sure I think it no shame.'

'I don't mean to harm you, nor yet for to scorn you,
One request I'll ask of you love where do you dwell.'
'I am a poor girl without friend or relation,
Besides I'm a hard-working factory girl.'

'Now love is a thing that does rule every nation;
Good morning kind sir and I hope you'll do well.
The hour is approaching from which I must leave you;
For I hear the dumb sound of yon factory bells.'

Now this poor girl she became a rich lady;
She married the squire of fame and renown.
She may bless the happy hour on the fine summer's morning,
That she first met the squire and on him did frown.

Now fill up your glasses and toast to these lasses,
That attends 'til the sound of yon factory bell.

## 42. Erin the Green

Draw near each young lover, give ear to my ditty,
That hears my sad mournful tale.
Come join me in concert, you'll lend to me your pity,
Whilst I my misfortune bewail.
The grief of my poor heart no tongue can disclose,
My cheeks are now pale that once bloomed like the rose.
It's all for a young man who I do suppose
Is now far from sweet Erin the green.

Oh when we were children, we walked out together
Along the green meadows so neat;
And although we were childish we loved one and other,
Whilst pulling the wild berries sweet.

131

It was in sweet Arvy we were sent to school,
He was first in his class and correct in each rule;
As I cheerfully walked home through sweet Kilnacoole,
With the flower of sweet Erin the green.

Oh his head on my bosom he used to repose it,
Each evening all under the shade.
A song in my praises my darling composed it,
And styled me the Coolederry Maid.
At the time that I denied him I'd die for his sake,
But little I thought my denial he'd take,
When to my misfortune I'd met a mistake
When he left me in Erin the green.

Oh sure I never thought that my darling would leave me,
No matter what I'd say or do;
And he oftimes told me he ne'er would deceive me,
But vowed to be constant and true;
But I need not blame him for breaking those laws,
For to my misfortune I myself was the cause,
And his truth and loyalty it'll gain him applause
When he's far from sweet Erin the green.

Come all you young maids of this dear Irish nation,
I beg you be steady and wise.
And likewise give air to my kind assertation,
And never your true love despise;
For such foolish folly, distracted I rave,
There's no place for me but yon dark silent grave,
And when all hope denied me I'll then take the leave
Of the flower of sweet Erin the green.

## 43. My Charming Edward Boyle

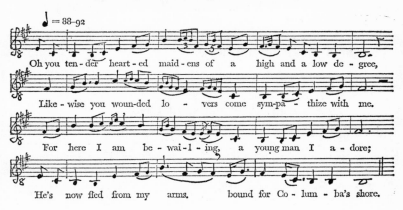

Oh you tender hearted maidens of a high and low degree,
Likewise you wounded lovers come sympathize with me.
For here I am bewailing a young man I adore;
He's now fled from my arms bound for Columba's [Columbia's]
shore.

In the county of Fermanagh in the parish of Rosslea,
In the townland of Grahwarren near the mountains of
Slievebeagh,
He was reared of honest parents and of St Patrick's soil;
But now they're sunk in sorrow for the loss of Edward Boyle.

Right well I do remember all in the month of May,
When Flora's flowery mantle decked the meadows gay.
When every thing seemed charming and blooms too, on her
smile,
I parted with my own true love, my charming Edward Boyle.

'Twas on a Monday morning his friends did him convey,
All from the town of Dundalk, from that round to the quay
With courage bold he did set sail and left the shamrock shore,
May all joys be with you Edward, will I ever see you more?

He was the pride of Collegelands, so well his flutes could play,
And the country is all lonesome since our Edward went away.
His comrades all both great and small, you'd swear they'd
leave their soil,
In hopes once more on Columba's [Columbia's] shore, for one
sight of young Edward Boyle.

## 44. The Banks of Clady

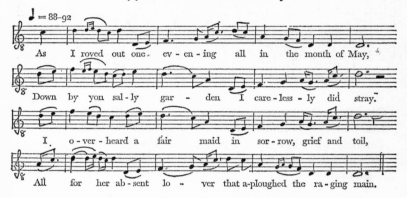

As I roved out one evening all in the month of May,
Down by yon sally garden I carelessly did stray.
I overheard a fair maid in sorrow grief and toil, [pain],
All for her absent lover that a-ploughed the raging main.

I boldly stepped it up to her, I gave her a surprise;
I own she did not know me for I being in disguise.
Said I, 'My blooming fair one, my joy and heart's delight,
How far do you mean to travel this dark and stormy night?'

'Kind sir, the way to Clady if you will be pleased to show.
Take pity all on a poor fair one, that knows not where 'til go,
In search of a fearless young man and Johnny is his name;
It's on the banks of Clady I'm told he does remain.'

'These are the banks of Clady, fair maid whereon you stand,
But do not trust young Johnny, for he's a false young man.

You do not trust young Johnny, for he'll not meet you here,
So trally with me to yon green woods no danger need you fear.'

'Oh if I had my Johnny here to-night he'd have freed me from
    all harm;
He's in the field of battle all in his uniform;
He's in the field of battle, his foes he does defy,
Like the royal King of Honour fought at the wars of Troy.'

'It is six long weeks and better since your Johnny left the
    shore,
To sail across the ocean, where the foaming billows roar;
To sail across the wide ocean, for honour and for gain,
But his ship was wrecked, all hands were lost, all on the coast
    of Spain.'

Oh when she heard that dreadful news she fell in deep despair,
'Til the wringing of her hands and the tearing of her hair.
'If my Johnny he lies drownéd no man on earth I'll take;
Through lonesome groves and valleys I'll wander for his sake.'

Oh when he saw her loyalty he could no longer stand.
He flew into her arms, saying, 'Betsy I'm the man!'
Saying, 'Betsy, lovely Betsy I'm the cause of all your pain,
And since we met on Clady Banks, Ah! we ne'er will part
    again.'

## 45. The Lass from Glasgow Town

Transposed up a semitone

Oh down by the Broom-i-law Bridge one eve-ning as I strayed,
When view-ing out some plea-sant ships I spied a char-ming maid;
And from her red and ro-sy cheeks the tears came cour-sing down;
I took her for a god-dess fair, the lass from Glas-gow town.

Oh down by the Broomilaw Bridge one evening as I strayed,
When viewing out some pleasant ships, I spied a charming
maid;
And from her red and rosy cheeks the tears came coursing
down;
I took her for a goddess fair, the lass from Glasgow town.

This young man says, 'My charming maid Ah! what detains
you here?'
'It's Ah! kind sir I'm waiting on a gallant sailor dear.
Three years ago he left me and for China he was bound,
And he said that he'd return again to the lass from Glasgow
town.'

Now this young man says, 'My charming maid it's useful for
to mourn,
For if he's three years gone from you he ne'er will back return.
Perhaps in battle he is slain or by the ocean drowned.'
'Oh! the Lord forbid,' replied the maid, the lass from Glasgow
town.

'For when young Willie left me he was beautiful and fair;
Red and rosy was his cheeks, cold yellow was his hair.
He enlisted with his majesty, and he's fighting for the Crown
He's fighting for his country or the lass from Glasgow town.'

Ah! this young man says, 'My charming maid, sad news I
    have to tell;
I was in your love's company when he in battle fell.
A cannonball proved his downfall as he lay on the ground,
And he begged of me for to protect the lass from Glasgow
    town.'

Oh! it's when she heard this dreadful news she fell in deep
    despair,
To the wringing of her hands and the tearing of her hair,
To the wringing of her hands till she fell on the ground,
And she begged of me for to protect the lass from Glasgow
    town.

## 46. Smith at Waterloo

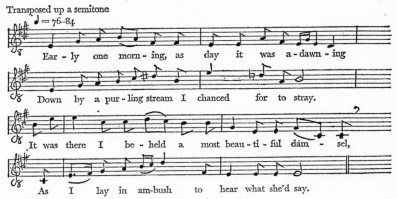

Early one morning, as day it was a-dawning
Down by a purling stream I chanced for to stray.
It was there I beheld a most beautiful damsel,
As I lay in ambush to hear what she'd say.

The song that she sang it would make the valleys ring;
The small birds and songsters around her did sing.
Saying, 'Is peace not proclaimed; is the war it not yet over;
Is my Willie not returning from famed Waterloo?'

Said I, 'My pretty fair maid, the pride of all nations,
Might I enquire of your true lover's name.

Perhaps your affections might shed on some other
And no longer ponder by this purling stream.'

'William Smith it is the name of this hero of fame,
And to him I must prove ever loyal and true.
For no other I'll enjoy but my own darling boy,
Yet my Willie's not returning from famed Waterloo.'

'If William Smith it be the name of this hero of fame,
It's with him I have spent sure many's the long campaign.
Through Portugal, Spain and France, where we both marched
    together
He was my chief comrade while marching through Spain.'

'It was then at Belgium, the French fleet they landed.
They fought like brave heroes and did them subdue.
They fought for three long days till at length they were
    defeated
By the brave noble forces at famed Waterloo.'

'There I saw him on the plains he lay bleeding and dying,
He scarcely got time for to bid me adieu.
And those were the last words I heard your Willie saying,
"Fare you well lovely Annie for ever adieu."'

Oh when that she heard of his sad declaration,
Her two rosy cheeks got as pale as the swan.
And when that he seen her in such a sad condition,
He flew into her arms saying, 'I am the man.'

'Here is the ring that between us were broken,
In the midst of all danger it reminds me of you,
Ah no other I'd enjoy but my own darling boy,
Saying your welcome lovely Willie from famed Waterloo.'

## 47. Texas Isle (2nd verse)

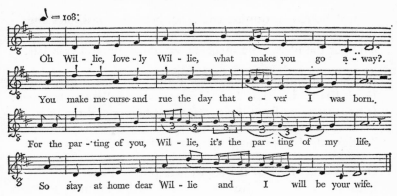

♩ = 108:

Oh Wil - lie, love - ly Wil - lie, what makes you go a - way?.

You make me curse and rue the day that e - ver I was born..

For the par - ting of you, Wil - lie, it's the par - ting of my life,

So stay at home dear Wil - lie and I will be your wife.

Oh farewell until my country 'til my parents I bid adieu,
And likewise 'til my own true love since I must part with you.
I'm listed with Her Majesty and I'll dress up in false style,
To join the British Army away down upon Texas Isle.

'Oh Willie, lovely Willie, what makes you go away?
You make me curse and rue the day that ever I was born,
For the parting of you, Willie, it's the parting of my life,
So stay at home dear Willie and I will be your wife.'

'Now Annie, lovely Annie, it is more than I can do,
For the Colonel has give orders and it's him we must obey.
He has ordered us out from Portsmouth for many's the weary
    long mile,
To fight the blacks and niggers away down upon Texas Isle.'

'Then we'll join our hands in wedlock band and I will be your
    bride,
I'll dress myself in man's apparel and I'll fight all by your
    side.
From Portsmouth quay we'll sail away, for many's the weary
    long mile,
And we'll fight the blacks and niggers away down upon Texas
    Isle.'

'Now Annie, lovely Annie, it is more nor you can do.
For your waist it is too slender and your fingers they are too
    fine.
Your delicate constitution could not bear that unwholesome
    clime,
To fight the blacks and niggers away down upon Texas Isle.'

Bad luck attend this cruel war and the hour that it first began
For it has robbed dear Ireland of many's a gallant young man.
It has tore them from their own sweet homes and the girls
    they left behind,
To fight the blacks and niggers away down upon Texas Isle.

Oh but when the war is over we will return home
Until our wives and sweethearts we'll pledge no more to roam,
But embrace them in our arms in that good old Irish style
And forget them blacks and niggers away down upon Texas Isle.

## 48. The Rocks of Giberaltar

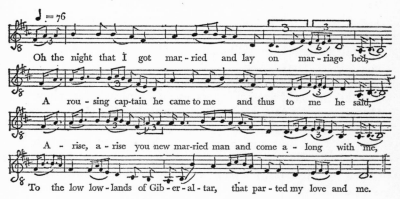

Oh the night that I got married and lay on marriage bed,
A rousing captain he came to me and thus to me he said,
'Arise, arise you new married man and come along with me,
To the low lowlands of Giberaltar, that parted my love and
    me.'

'Lie still my bonny wee lass, lie still and take your rest,
For I must go with this young man and fight for my
    counteree.
Now I must go with this young man and fight for my liberty.'
It's the rocks of bonny Giberaltar that parts my love and me.

Oh no ribbons I'll wear round my neck, nor comb run through
    my hair,
Nor stay fasten around my waist 'til show my figure fair.
No candle in my room at night, that used to burn so free,
Since the rocks of bonny Giberaltar has parted my love and
    me.

## 49. The Old Oak Tree

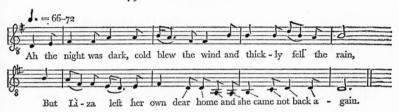

Ah the night was dark, cold blew the wind and thickly fell the
    rain,
But Lisa left her own dear home and she came not back again.

Oh she was young and fair to see, but love had made her bold,
That very night at twelve o'clock beneath the old oak tree.

Ah that very night at ten o'clock, beneath the old oak tree
She promised James her ain true love that with him she would
    be.

She heeded not the drenching rain, nor the tempest's threatening
    roar,
She threw her cloak all round her and walked quickly from the
    door.

That night rolled on and morning came and yet she was not
    home;

And much it grieved her friends to think how this that she would
roam.

Her mother started out and she cried an ancient while,
Saying, 'I will search the kingdom, or I'll find my darling
child.'

For three long dreary weeks she spent searching the country
round,
'Til her journey proved of no avail for Liza was not found.

And how to reach her lonely home, grieving woe and widow
tried,
Then crushed with grief she then laid down and broken-
hearted died.

Near 'til the scene of all the woe, was the owner of the ground
Young Squire Cohen came one day to hunt with all his
hounds.

Up hill, down dale they hotly rode, with a gallant company,
Till as by chance they lost the fox beneath the old oak tree.

It was there the dogs began to yelp and snuff and tear the clay.
Not all the horn nor whip could do wouldn't drive them
hounds away.

The gentlemen they gathered round, they called for pick and
spade.
They dug the ground and there they found that missing
murdered maid.

Ah her bosom was so dazzling fair, all black with wounds and
blows;
And from the cut fresh blood gushed forth and trinkled down
her clothes.

Ah the grave to show that horrid work it was a dreadful sight,
To see the worms eat through her eyes, that once was blue
and bright.

And in her side a knife was stuck, all to her grief and shame,
When the gentlemen all on the haft read Squire Cohen's
name.

'I have done the deed,' young Cohen cried, 'my soul it's fit
for hell;
You hide her cold corpse from my sight and I the truth will
tell.'

'Oh yes I loved Eliza long, all by a villiant heart,
I won her to my vicious ways, triumphant o'er her heart.'

'And on this she teased till I grew tired until it seemed to me
That the devil whispers take her life, and then you shall go
free.'

'Oh the knife I did my dinner cut, I plunged it through her
breast;
And with the haft I knocked her down I need not tell the
rest.'

'And from that dreadful hour to this she stands before my
eyes.
I can always see her bleeding ghost and can hear her dying
cries.'

It was there he stood and cast upon that corpse a look of pain,
He took a pistol from his breast and he fire it through his
brain.

Oh he was buried where he fell, no Christian grave got he;
There was no one found to bless the ground beneath the old
oak tree.

## 50. The Wee Croppy Tailor

𝅘𝅥𝅭 = 60-66.

'Oh in Lon - don's fair ci - ty there dwelt a great dame,

For fame, birth nor breed - ing none can her ex - ceed.

'She's a black - sm - ith's daugh - ter, and her story to tell

That her hus - band he must be a troo - - - per.

Oh in London's fair city there dwelt a great dame,
For fame, birth nor breeding none can her exceed.
She's a blacksmith's daughter, and her story to tell
That her husband he must be a trooper.

There was an elegant tailor lived next door by
And on that fair damsel he soon cast an eye.
He swore 'pon his sould that with her he would lie,
For he didn't give a damn for the trooper.

Ah this tailor came to this fair lady one night
He called her his dear, his joy and delight.
'Ten guineas I'll give you for my lodging this night,
For I know that your husband's on duty.'

'Oh yes Mr Tailor and your very right,
When you know that my husband's on duty;
But sure if he comes home he will give you a fright
That will put you in mind of the trooper.'

When the bargain was over all finished and done,
They both went to bed, and the spree it began.
When the spree was all over they both fell asleep
But they minded no more of the trooper.

Ah the trooper came home in the middle o' the night
He rapped at the door and he give them a fright.
'Oh hide me, oh hide me,' the tailor he cries,
'For I hear the bold knocks of the trooper.'

'Oh there's an old useless cupboard that stands by the door
And in it you'll be safe, snug and secure.
I will trip down the stairs and I'll open the door
And I'll let in my husband the trooper.'

Oh with kindness and compliments oh to be sure
She tripped down the stairs and she opened the door.
'For your kindness and compliments I don't give a damn
Come light me a fire,' says the trooper.

'Oh husband dear husband there's no fire stuff,
You get into your bed you'll be warm enough.'
'There's an old useless cupboard that stands by the door,
I'll burn it this night,' says the trooper.

'Oh husband dear husband grant me one desire,
That old useless cupboard's too good for the fire,
And it's in it I rear a game-cock I admire,'
'I must see your game cock,' says the trooper.

Ah the trooper walked forward and opened the door
Here gets the wee tailor safe, snug and secure.
He hauled him out to the middle o' the floor,
'Or is this your game-cock?' says the trooper.

'Oh now Mr Tailor you're a very cunning fox
When did you become one of my wife's game-cocks?
For that very same reason I'll give you a knock
That will put you in mind of the trooper.'

He caught hold of the tailor just by the two ears;
He clean cut them off with his own little shears.
For the night's diversion he paid very dear
So away went the wee croppy tailor.

## 51. James Magee

Oh James Magee they do call me, the same I won't deny;
Far from my house and country I was obliged to fly,
For the sake of houses and free land my aunt against me
  swore,
But now I must prepare to sail far far from Innishmore.

My father and my mother died, I had one aunt alive,
She married an Orangeman and with him did contrive,
That if he'd swear my life away it's a hanged I might be,
And then she'd fall the only heir of all my property.

Ah the morning of my trial on the green table she swore,
This is the man and the leading man of six thousand men or
  more;
This is the man that did the wrong and now of him take hold,
For on Wednesday night at twelve o'clock my husband's gun
  he stole.

'Oh aunt,' says I, 'don't perjured be lest injured I might be,
For on the great tribunal day when the Lord will on us call,
We'll have no false judge or jury for one God, He'll judge us
  all.'

The cruel judge made answer and unto me did say,
'I can do nothing for you, she swore so bitterly.
I can do nothing for you, she has swore your life away,
So now you must prepare to sail, you're bound for New South
  Wales.'

It is not my long sail troubles me nor yet my distant voyage,
It's the parting of my children small that have not come to age,
That the curse on me and my poor wife and my three children
    small
May it light all on you, Kate McCabe, my aunt I should you
    call.

Once I had a well-furnished house no room could it afford,
To enter in an Orangeman, when he'd be on record,
But if a Ribbonman would call that way, well treated he would
    be,
Ah but now there does not dwell a man where dwelt young
    James Magee.

## 52. The Murder of William Funston

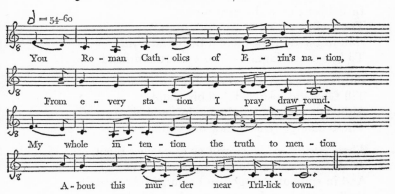

You Roman Catholics of Erin's nation,
From every station I pray draw round,
My whole intention the truth to mention,
About this murder near Trillick town.

On the ninth of March it will be long remembered,
It being the fair-day of Irvinestown,
When William Funston was home returning
His corpse next morning on the road was found.

The news was spread without hesitation,
That great transaction had come to light.
They did transpire, these boys Maguire
Was in Funston's company on that unlucky night.

The case was tested, they were arrested,
To Omagh jailhouse they were conveyed.
Two purgéd Orangemen named Smith and Armstrong
To swear against them was highly paid.

In Omagh jailhouse they stood their trial,
Where they stood handcuffed there hand to hand;
And their consolation was their aged father,
With a heart undaunted in the dock did stand.

When I heard the story of that man McGrory,
The sight that morning that he did see
Was the corpse of Funston, on the back of Armstrong,
'Til rob and murder they did agree.

In Belfast city at the next assizes,
They will be tried as we understand;
And in Sandy Row there'll be found a jury
To hang the Maguires with a heart and hand.

But here success attend our Roman jurors,
Till God and justice did nobly stand.
Although they were only few in number,
These Orange tyrants they did command.

Their purgéd evidence will ne'er convict them,
That day it's gone since O'Connell's time;
And in spite of Orangemen or purgéd Armstrong
We'll shout hurrah! you are welcome home.

## 53. The Country I Was Born In

I have just left Donegal, when I thought I'd give a call,
It's always what becomes an honest neighbour,
I am going far away bound for Amerikey,
Where I'm told a man he's paid there for his labour.

It is there I'll see ochone all the men I knew at home,
That I often times drank with until morning;
But no matter where I roam I will always think of home,
For old Ireland's the country I was born in.

So now strike up your bands in the praise of Ireland,
Though I'm going far away from it in the morning;
But no matter where I roam I will always think of home,
For old Ireland's the country I was born in.

It is many's a wearied mile I have walked through Erin's
    Isle,
And so many are the hardships I have seen.
I have saw both young and old a-starving in the cold,
Oh when hurled by the landlord from their door.

But thank God that is past and that I have seen the last,
May the wrongs of dear old Ireland be righted.
Oh God grant that we may see old Ireland proud and free,
It is if her sons were only once united.

So now cheer up your bands in the praise of Ireland,
Though I'm going far away from it in the morning.
And no matter where I roam I'll always think of home
For old Ireland's the country I was born in.

It is now I say goodbye for the time is drawing nigh,
And our steamer's leaving Queenstown tomorrow.
My luggage it is light, my purse is very bright,
My heart it is loaded down with sorrow.

For now I must set sail from you poor old 'Granuweel',
As thousands of my people done before me.
For if I could stay at home, abroad I'd never roam,
But I cannot boys, where is the man can blame me?

So now strike up your bands in the praise of Ireland,
Though I'm going far away from it in the morning.
But no matter where I roam I will always think of home,
For Ireland's the country I was born in.

## 54. Pat O'Donnell

Transposed up a tone

♩ = 63

My name is Pat O' Don-nell and I came from Don-e-gal.
I am yo-u know a dead-ly foe to trai-tors one and all;
For the shoo-ting of James Ca-rey I was tried in Lon-don town,
And on that fa-tal scaf-fold my life I must lay down.

My name is Pat O'Donnell and I came from Donegal,
I am you know a deadly foe to traitors one and all;
For the shooting of James Carey I was tried in London town,
And on that fatal scaffold my life I must lay down.

I stepped on board the *Melrose*, in August eighty-three,
And on my voyage to Capetown he was unknown to me.
When I heard this was Carey there was angry words and blows,
And the villain he strove to take my life on board of the
    Melrose.

I stood up to my own defence, to fight before I'd die,
A pocket pistol I drew forth and at him I let fly.
The second volley I let go it touched his treacherous heart,
And I give him the third rally boys, before he did us part.

Mrs Carey and her son came down to the cabin where he lay,
And when they seen him in his corpse it filled them with
    dismay.
'O'Donnell you shot my husband,' Mrs Carey loud did cry,
'I did it to my own defence, kind madam', then said I.

The sailors had me handcuffed in strong irons I lay bound,
They give me o'er a prisoner when I landed in Capetown.
They brought me back to London, my trial for to stand,
And the prosecutors for the crime were Carey's wife and son.

For wilful murder I was tried and guilty found at last,
The jury found the verdict and the judge the sentence passed.
The jury found the verdict and the learned judge did cry,
'On the twentieth of September Pat O'Donnell you must die.'

Oh if I had've been a free man and could live another year,
All traitors and informers before me'd shake with fear.
As St Patrick drove the serpents from our sainted Irish ground,
I would make them fly before me like the hare before the
    hounds.

Adieu, adieu to Donegal, the place where I was born,
Likewise to the United States where they ne'er held me with
    scorn.
Adieu, adieu to Donegal and I hope that you will see,
The Saxon driven from the soil and the green flag waving free.

## 55. The Burning of Rosslea

(From the singing of Nelly Mullarky)

On a fine Monday morning about eight o'clock,
The B's of Rosslea sure they got a great shock.
When Lister was popped boys they made no delay,
But sent out dispatches, ri-tor-al-aye-ay.

From Cooneen to Ballagh, and from that down to Crom,
From Inver and Shanro, and the robbers from Drum.
They all marched in sections to the town of Rosslea,
To put a full stop to ri-tor-al-aye-ay.

The Clough boys assembled outside the church gate,
They seemed in a hurry for fear of being late.
But the head of these B-Men said, 'What shall we say,
If we meet with the rebels singing tor-al-aye-ay?'

At the centre of the town sure the work did begin,
To see them burning down houses, you'd think it a sin.
But the most of their bullets they all went astray,
For they hadn't the tips of ri-tor-al-aye-ay.

They roamed through the town like a pack of wild boars,
They broke all the windows and hammered the doors.
They pillaged and looted and carried away,
The stuff of poor Catholics, ri-tor-al-aye-ay.

On that very night month and just in the same year,
The 'Volunteers' met boys, without the least fear.
Three houses they burned for each one in Rosslea,
All done to the tune of ri-tor-al-aye-ay.

Some of the boys on the run had to go,
They travelled the mountains through frost and in snow.
But they're at home and at home they will stay,
And they never stop singing ri-tor-al-aye-ay.

# Appendix 3

# Song notes

## Abbreviations

EFS  *The Penguin Book of English Folk Songs*, Ralph Vaughan Williams and A. L. Lloyd (eds), Penguin, Harmondsworth, 1971.

FSU  *Folksongs Sung in Ulster*, Robin Morton, Mercier Press, Cork, 1970.

GG  *Folksongs of the North-east*, Gavin Greig, Folklore Associates, Hatboro, Pennsylvania, 1963.

ISB  *Irish Street Ballads*, Colm O'Lochlainn, Three Candles Press, Dublin, 1962.

MISB  *More Irish Street Ballads*, Colm O'Lochlainn, Three Candles Press, Dublin, 1968.

MB  *Marrow Bones: English Folksongs from the Hammond and Gardiner MSS.*, Frank Purslow, EFDSS Publications, London, 1965.

SHC  'Sam Henry Collection', typescript, Belfast Central Library.

JO  *Bothy Songs and Ballads*, ed. John Ord, Alexander Gardner Ltd, Paisley, 1930.

## Chapter 1

*1. Molly Bawn Lowry*

This was a great favourite among nineteenth-century ballad-sheet publishers but the story is a very old one indeed, though the one we have now is much less exotic than the old European versions. Molly Bawn is an enchanted woman who changes form with the setting of the sun. However, tradition has rationalized this 'magic' element away, making her death one of mistaken identity with Molly sheltering from the rain. Half concealed under a bush with her apron drawn over her head it would be easy to take her for a swan.

Often some magical quality still remains with Molly's ghost returning to secure her love's acquittal; John's version however omits this and also he does not have the common verse, which notes the pleasure of the other girls in the area at Molly's death because 'She shone above them like a mountain of snow'.

In *Ulster Folklife*, vol. 17, 1971 (Some 'Songs and Ballads in use in the province of Ulster . . . 1845') Hugh Shields makes some interesting tenuous suggestions as to the origin of this song. See also ISB, song 29. The tune is of course the one often used for 'Lord Gregory'.

### 2. *Columbia the Free*
I have met many Irishmen in exile and almost without exception they have effused poetic on Mother Ireland – great people, great country, great times.

No matter where they go, Shepherd's Bush to Melbourne, an idealized Ireland is carried around inside them. I met one marvellous man in a Camden Town pub who talked at length about his ideal, but in reply to my query as to how often he went home to Kerry he said, 'Ah well I havn't been back now for thirty years.' Perhaps it is for the best, but I can't help wondering if he wrote this song?

### 3. *Willie's Ghost (fragment)*
This is only a fragment of a version of 'The Grey Cock' or 'The Lover's Ghost' see F. J. Child, *The English and Scottish Popular Ballads*, Dover Books, New York, 1965 (paperback), p. 248. The tune used here is close to the one used by Mrs Cecilia Costello of Birmingham (see EFS, p. 52). It would seem to be an open question as to whether or not the revenant is an intrusion on the song, but there is no doubt that the 'night visiting' idea and the fleeing ghost seem to have been cemented fairly fully by the tradition.

With regard to the rest of the song, I have in my possession a nineteenth-century broadsheet entitled 'Willy O!', and when I read it to John he said that it was this song that his mother used to sing. Here is the text as per the broadsheet. (For another close text see 'Folk Ballads from Donegal and Derry', collected by Hugh Shields, Leader Records, LEA 4055.)

> Come all young maids that's fair and handsome
> While in vain your tears do flow,
> For my love I'm daily weeping,
> He is my charming Willy O.
>
> My love he's gone on board of the tender,
> Where to find him I do not know,
> May kind providence still protect him,
> And send me back my Willy O.

Had I the gold of West Indies,
Or all the silver in Mexico,
I would give it all to the Queen of England,
If she would grant me my Willy O.

As Mary lay sleeping, her true love came creeping,
To her bed-chamber door so slow,
Saying rise up, rise up lovely Mary,
For I am your own true Willy O.

Mary rose and put on her clothes
To her chamber door did go,
It's there she found her own true love,
And his face as white as snow.

Willy dear where is the blushes,
That you had some years ago
O Mary dear, the day has changed them
For I am the ghost of your Willy O.

Those seven long years I am daily writing
To the Bay of Biscay O,
But cruel death sent me no answer,
From my charming Willy O.

They spent that night in deep discoursing,
Concerning their courtship some time ago,
They kissed, shook hands with sorrow parting,
Just as the cock began to crow.

Although my body lies in West Indies,
My ghost shall guard you, and,
So farewell jewel, since we are for parting,
Since I'm no more your Willy O.

When she saw him disappearing,
Down her cheeks the tears did flow,
Mary dear, sweetheart and darling,
Weep no more for your Willy O.


*4. Behind Yon Blue Mountain*
I can't tell you anything about this song in praise of lovely Tyrone and
its females. But some of its lines I find particularly effective:

Its lakes may go dry and its streams cease to moan,
Before I forget of you lovely Tyrone.

*5. Lovely Jane from Enniskea*
Here is another one of the many 'broken-token songs' where lovers
being separated break or exchange something like a medal or a ring
as a token of love separated but not ended. However this one does not
seem fully to fit the pattern because usually when the lover returns he
knows his old girlfriend, though he pretends not to. He then goes on
to test her loyalty by trying to seduce her, as she does not seem to
recognize him. When she maintains her loyalty he admits his identity
and she in turn welcomes him home with great relief. (See 'The
Banks of Claudy', song 2 *FSU.*, and appendix 2, songs 43, 45 and
46.) If I had been her I would have blackened his eye for such a
mean deceit.

In 'Lovely Jane from Enniskea' our young man really does know his
girlfriend. So my immediate response was to think the better of him for
it. However when I think about it I wonder if his attempted seduction
is any more acceptable just because he doesn't know his love. I wonder
why she accepts his disloyalty so readily?

John thinks that the Enniskea referred to in the song is in Co. Down.
However I don't think there is a townland called Enniskea in that county
but there is certainly one in Co. Louth, which is south of the border
and the county immediately south of Down. Enniskea is to be found
between the border and Dundalk and a factor which would support this
location is that it is near Ravensdale. In the song this is called Ravensvale
but this may, and probably is, a mistake. The tune is the same as is
generally used for 'The Rocks of Bawn' and also used for 'The Maid
of Magheracloon' (song 6).

*6. The Maid of Magheracloon*
This song seems to be very well known in Co. Fermanagh. I have a very
similar version from neighbours of John, Nelly and Peter Mullarkey
(*FSU*, song 21,) and I have heard many other people in the area
singing it.

The tune is basically the same as that used here for 'Lovely Jane from
Enniskea', which in turn is very close to that generally used for 'The
Rocks of Bawn' (*ISB*, song 23). Magheracloon is a parish in Co.
Monaghan, near that county's border with Cavan.

## Chapter 2

*7. The Pony Song (fragment)*
Here John remembers just a snatch of a song from his school days. The
words and the tune obviously belong to 'Jingle Bells', but both have
been adapted – the last line makes it 'belong' to that area.

## 8. Tom Kelly's Cow

I cannot really add anything to the explanation in the text of how this song came to be written. The whole idea appeals to my sense of humour and should serve as a warning to any young girl on the dangers of strong drink. See what happened to Tommy Kelly's Cow!

A lot of poteen was made in this area at one time and I think you might get a drop yet if you know the right people! John gives us much information about the making of poteen in chapter 4 and for the fascinating social and economic background to what was once the industry of illicit distillation I recommend the relevant chapter in K. H. Connell, *Irish Peasant Society*, Oxford University Press, 1968. Indeed the whole book has much relevance to a fuller appreciation of the story told herein.

## 9. The Molly Maguires

This is one of the few songs that John wrote himself. He wrote some others but he does not remember any more. It seems that they were mostly 'comics' about local factions, and as you could get into trouble very easily he tended not to sing them and thus has forgotten them.

Tradition has it that the Molly Maguires were formed in the early nineteenth-century after the Catholic neighbours of a Co. Tyrone widow, Molly Maguire, had successfully foiled an attempt to evict her. This success spurred them to combine to carry out similar defensive action in other areas.

I find John's song somewhat confusing for various reasons. In the first verse we find the Mollys in conflict with Defenders. Now the Defenders were an organization formed in the late eighteenth-century to act as a defence for Catholics against Peep O' Day Boys (Protestant) attacks. Of course this verse may point to the fact that, especially in Fermanagh, there seems always to have been much fighting between the Catholic factions, perhaps because there is no great Orange threat to deal with. Some families have been split by this factionalism and neighbours are often at daggers drawn. However, this intra-Catholic tension does not fit in with implication of the last line of verse two. This would suggest some friendly relationship between the more aggressive and extreme Ribbonmen and the Molly Maguires. It is certain that no such relationship ever existed and many clashes at local fairs can be catalogued. The Molly's tended to join the Ancient Order of Hiberians, when it began to gain wider influence in the early years of the new century, and backed the treaty setting up the Irish Free State in 1921. The Ribbonmen melted into more extreme organizations and the tension continues.

## 10. Hunting Song (fragment)

The whole of Co. Fermanagh is a great area for hunting, but it is not the side-saddled sport of the lords and squires and those who would emulate them. This is the sport of the farmer, with his wellington-boots, working clothes and his couple of beagles. Out they go every Saturday morning in autumn to hunt the hare on foot. All day they climb ditches and over hills and round bogs, and end up in the evening at the pub to 'warm themselves' and sing a song or two.

Each area will usually have its own hunting song and all tend to be a list of the virtues of the local dogs and the hare. Don't forget the hare – huntsmen are as proud of their good hares as they are of their dogs. This fragment that John gives us is no exception to the rule and it is obviously part of a particularly good song. The tune is a fine one as well.

### 11. The Follom Brown-Red

Cockfighting was in evidence in ancient India, China and Persia. It seems to have travelled to Britain via Greece and Rome then across Europe, probably arriving in these islands before Caesar. In spite of various attempts to repress it (and it has been illegal in Great Britain since 1849), it is still practised certainly in Ireland, especially in the more remote areas.

Much effort is put into the breeding and training of cocks, and of course much money is made and lost in wagers. Hard-boiled eggs and chopped meat seem to be favoured foods and many exercises are used to strengthen their muscles. The bird is usually kept for one or two years before being 'pitted' and his body is constantly dressed with an ammonia solution in order to toughen the skin. In preparation for 'a main' (a battle) his wings are clipped and hackle and rump feathers are clipped close and the comb is trimmed. Each breeder will probably have a number of birds, but for security reasons these are 'walked' (brought up and trained by) various people throughout the area.

Normally 'the main' consists of battles between an agreed number of pairs, the majority deciding who wins 'the main'. At one time the birds fought to the death but it would now seem that a badly wounded cock can be withdrawn at any time. I certainly have seen a cock that was beaten strutting round a farmyard. I asked about it and was told that it had put up a good fight; though it would never be 'pitted' again it was being kept as a pet.

There are two other types of 'main'. The Battle Royal, where a number of birds are pitted at the same time and the winner is the one who remains at the end to crow. The other is a sort of a knock-out competition where a number of pairs battle and the winners of each are pitted against each other, until only two winners remain to fight for the championship.

Many cockfights take place in the area of the border separating the 'six counties' from Eire. The idea is that if the police from one side or the other try to interfere then the participants can simply move over to the other side of the boundary, thus leaving their assailants' jurisdiction. In the past some co-operation has been attempted by the RUC and the Guards (Eire police), one moving in from one side and one from the other. However, the warning system seems to be very good and I certainly don't know of any recent court action.

Of course, the problems of the 'cockers' will have become more difficult lately with increased action along both sides of the border because of the recent 'troubles'. I have been told of at least one 'main' interrupted by an army helicopter. So you see it is true when our politicians say that 'all sections of our society are affected by the recent disorders.'

## Chapter 3

### 12. Sergeant Neill

I did try to find out when the knapsack sprayer was introduced into Ireland, without any success. John tells me that it was sometime in the early 1920s that Sergeant Neill began his business enterprise. However, he thinks that it was being used at an earlier date in other parts of the country.

Nicknames or alternative names are still used very much in the county, presumably for the reasons that John gives in his story. Some of them show great imagination and one wonders on what they are based. Names like Paddy 'Faddley', Tom 'the Gate' 'Springheel Jack' read like names from a Fellini film.

### 13. John Barleygrain

The myth of the King Corn, killed but risen again, can be traced back through the ages to the Pharaohs. Whether or not (as Vaughan Williams and Lloyd wonder in *EFS*) the song as we know it is the creation of some proselytizing antiquarian which has been taken over by 'the folk' is only of academic interest. The song now has a strong life of its own and has taken vigorous root in the traditional repertory of these islands.

When I asked John if he knew any songs about harvest or suchlike, he came up with this fragment of the song that his father had sung. The next time I went down to see him he sang me a complete but different version. I wondered if he had remembered it since I was last there. No, he had remembered that there was a man (a good singer) down the road who used to sing it and John went to see him. I tell this story to give some more insight into the wonderful spirit of John Maguire, but also to show that within a few miles of each other two very distinct versions of the one song had existed, as if in isolation.

I decided that we could not really call this second version part of John's repertoire as given to me, because I had stimulated him to learn it. However, it has been included in appendix 1 as John sings it. Needless to say, I have also been to see the man John had it from and have recorded him singing it. A comparison of the two singing the one song has been of help to Professor Blacking and I would like to thank Frank Murphy, John's source, for carrying the song. As I have said, the song took vigorous root in the 'tradition' and many versions are available both on record and in print (Folkways records, FM4052, 'Irish and British Songs from the Ottawa Valley'; and FW8871, 'Field Trip England'. See *EFS* p. 56, and *ISB*, song 89).

### 13A. *John Barleygrain*

'Transposed up a semitone

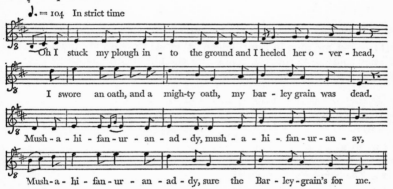

$\quad$ = 104 In strict time

Oh I stuck my plough into the ground and I heeled her overhead,
I swore an oath, and a mighty oath, my barleygrain was dead.
Mush-a-hi-fan-ur-an-addy, mush-a-hi-fan-ur-an-ay,
Mush-a-hi-fan-ur-an-addy, sure the barleygrain's for me.

When the snow and the frost was over and the dew began to fall,
The barleygrain it peeped up its head and it made a lad of them all.

CHORUS

Oh the mower came with his big scythe, he cut me off my feet;
And they done worse and ten times worse they tied me like a thief.

CHORUS

The binder come with her big thumb and on me she did frown,
But in my middle she got a thistle, that pulled her courage down.

CHORUS

Oh the thresher came with his big flail and on me he did frown;
And he done worse and ten times worse, he turned me upside down.

CHORUS

Ah they put me then in linen sacks and placed me in a well;
They left me there for a day or two till my belly began to swell.

CHORUS

Oh they put me then on linen sheets and spread me to and fro;
They left me there for a day or two till my beard began to grow.

CHORUS

They placed me on the kiln-head, took the marrow out of my bones,
And they done worse and ten times worse, they ground me a-tween two
stones.

CHORUS

They put me then in punchers and they sent me up the town,
They sold me to the McManus', for the bill of fifty pounds.

CHORUS

Oh they drank me in the kitchen and they drank me in the hall,
And they done worse and ten times worse, they lashed me against the
wall.

CHORUS

## 14. The Strabane Hiring Fair
I can't really add anything to what John has said about the hiring fairs,
nor do I need to.

Both Biddy and Brian, John's sister and brother, sing this song though
it seems to be an unspoken rule that neither of the two men sing it in
Biddy's company – it is *her* song. The tune is the first part of a much
used melody usually known as 'The Peeler and the Goat'.

## 15. Thousands Are Sailing to America
As John says, this was a 'ballad' and so one would expect it to have fairly
wide currency and indeed I have heard it sung in Co. Clare. The tune
is the first part of a double jig though I'm afraid I have never heard its
name.

This is a song from the 1880s, by which time the enforced emigration
of famine times had become a ritual, almost part of growing up. Emigration by this time was institutionalized and this song has about it an air
of resignation. It seems to say 'We don't want you to leave, but go you

will. After all emigration is part of our life, we cannot expect anything else.' . . . And thousands are still sailing to America.

### 16. Fee and Flannigan

John Flannigan disappeared on 16 April 1903, the same day as he had drawn a substantial amount of money from his bank. It was assumed that he had left the country. Seven months later a body was found, buried in a dung-heap, near to slaughter-houses owned by the Fee family of Clones. The person had obviously been murdered; the hands and legs were tied, the skull smashed and the throat cut. Beside the body was found a butchering knife, belonging to young Joseph Fee. On this evidence Fee was arrested and placed on remand.

He was tried in Monaghan, at both the spring and summer assizes, but on both occasions the juries disagreed. However, he was re-tried in Belfast in December 1904, found guilty and was hanged on the 22nd of that month. Fee never wavered in his protestations of innocence, though local folklore has it that he whispered a confession to Pierrepont, the hangman, just before his execution. This rumour may of course be based on fact. However, one could offer various reasons why such a rumour would be psychologically necessary to the community, all of which relate to the need of a society to be 'right' in taking such extreme action as 'killing' someone.

The song is a straightforward narrative, typical of songs of 'dastardly doings', though now the chronology of events has obviously become confused. It is interesting to note that Fee's rumoured confession of guilt is also implied in the last verse, where, properly penitent, the criminal asks the forgiveness of the community. This again is typical of this kind of ballad.

I would like to thank the Rev. Peadar Livingstone of Castleblaney for the factual information embodied in this note.

### 17. The Constant Farmer's Son

Here again are all the elements of a 'ballad'. Murder, heartbreak, just desert, etc., etc. It also seems to be widely known. It was known down in West Clare and Una Woods, a singer friend, has collected a version, substantially the same as John's, from travelling people in England. It also has much in common with 'Bruton town'. Not only is the story-line similar, but it shares verses like the one where the distraught woman covers her dead lover's body with leaves. (See *English Folksongs*, Cecil J. Sharp, Novello, 1959, p. 2; also 'In Seaport Town', in *English Folksongs from the Southern Appallachians*, Oxford University Press, 1960, vol. 1, p. 310. There is an almost identical text in vol. 1 of the *Journal of the Folksong Society*, p. 160, under the same title.)

*18. Young Mary from Kilmore*

Based on the pastourelle theme, this song has the stamp of the school-master's pen or some other 'learned' versifier. I am not sure of the significance of verse 4, that is the one that names the heroes. At first I thought it might be an intrusion but I have the song from another source in the same area and the same verse is included, which tends to suggest that it has some part to play. Certainly the names, especially Gunn and Maguire, have strong Fermanagh ties.

The second version I have is sung to the same tune and is exactly the same song, except that the singer misses out John's third verse, but replaces it with this verse which John seems to have forgotten:

And besides young man what do I care for your houses and free land?
I would feel a deal more pleasure in rambling round the strand;
Where the small birds sing on branch and spray and the lark she joins in corps,
And where Pheobus beams at the dawn of day, on the lake of sweet Kilmore.

Another slight difference is that the teller of the story in John's song is John O'Brien whereas the other version identifies him as John Smith, a much more anonymous figure.

## Chapter 4

*19. My Charming Mary*

This is one of the first songs John gave me and his singing of it convinced me, at that very early stage, that here was a very fine singer indeed. You can hear for yourself on the companion record to this volume. The tune, a version of 'Anac Chuan', flows along like a stream and carries the words like eddying leaves. I hope that doesn't seem too gushing but I think this is a really beautiful song, well sung.

*20. Joe Higgins*

Otherwise known as 'I don't mind if I do', this will be found in print in one of Walton's latter-day chapbooks, published in Dublin (*New Treasury of Irish Songs and Ballads*, Part I, p. 148). It was probably a fairly popular ballad-sheet at one time, and was likely sung on the music-hall stage. However Joe Higgins certainly left his mark on it in the Rosslea area. By relating it to himself he made it his song. He seems to have been a bit of a rake and probably enjoyed 'shocking' the neighbours with this gently bawdy song.

*21 Bold Jack Donohue*
There are many songs about the forerunner of Ned Kelly though this one, probably carried on a ballad-sheet, seems to be the most common. His story is very much as given in the text though various reasons are given for his transportation. As he was transported in 1825 there is reason to doubt that his crime was 'being a bold United boy', but be that as it may, he soon became a 'bushranger' and indeed was sentenced to death twice by the same court. On his way from the court to jail in 1828 he slipped the chains and began the career that was to make him a folk hero in much the same league as Robin Hood or Jesse James. His activities ended abruptly in September 1830 but he has lived on in the ballads.

John Meredith and Hugh Anderson, in *Folksongs of Australia*, Ure Smith, Sydney; Horwitz Group Books, London, 1967, quote two texts (p. 63 and 97). The latter, collected in northern New South Wales, apart from minor differences, is the same as the one given here, except that it has a chorus. You will notice that John misses a line in verse six. According to the text in Meredith and Anderson it is the second line and they give it as: 'For I'll fight this night with all my might, cried Bold Jack Donohue'.

For those of you especially interested in outlaw songs in general and this one in particular may I refer you to Maureen Jolliffe, *The Third Book of Irish Ballads*, Mercier Press, 1971, song 20, where the editor offers much fascinating background material on Donohue.


*22. The Gauger's Song*
The Gaugers were the Revenue Police, who, until the newly formed RIC (Royal Irish Constabulary) took over their duties in 1855, were charged with the suppression of illicit distillation. The world and his neighbour 'run a drop' in the first half of the nineteenth century. The small farmer made it to pay his rent and there are many examples of the gentry and even the priesthood making it – presumably because they liked it. Certainly if we are to accept contemporary reports the legal 'parliament whiskey' was difficult to get, and was even harder to swallow.

The second half of the century saw the 'problem' diminish greatly. The priesthood, who increasingly came from among the ordinary people, knew only too well the problems attendant on 'drink' and began to preach against it often making it a reserved sin (that is, one for which one must approach the bishop for absolution). The RIC seem to have been more effective, and perhaps less corrupt, than their forerunners and finally the more secure position of the tenant, in the later years of the century, made illicit distillation much less of a financial necessity.

It is interesting to note, however, that during the recent 'troubles' in Belfast and Derry there seems to have been a resurgence of the trade. Another version is to be found in SHC, song 103. Geoff Wood, from Leeds, has a version from Letterkenny, Co. Donegal, almost identical to John's though it has a short 'Whack fol the, etc.' chorus and the tune is a different one.

### 23 The Mountain Dew (fragment)

John says about this song, 'I believe maybe that was all of that song that poor old Jemmy was fit to sing at that time anyway.' In fact, there seems only to be one more verse anyway. The version given here is very close to that in *The Clancy Brothers and Tommy Makem Songbook*, Tiparm Music, 1964, p. 28. You can hear the McPeakes sing a somewhat different one on Topic 12T87.

## Chapter 5

### 24. Lough Ooney

Lough Ooney or Lough Oona is well shrouded from the public view just off the main road between Clones and the county town of Monaghan, but I'm afraid I can tell little more about this song. The classical allusions would tend to suggest the pen of some latter-day hedge school-master.

I find the tune a particularly pleasant one and it is basically the same one used by another singer in the more western parts of Co. Fermanagh.

### 25. The Handsome Collier Lad

A. L. Lloyd has quoted a text close to this in *Folksong in England*, Panther, 1969, p. 356, under the title of 'Johnny Seddon.' The more complete 'vagueness' of the text given here would seem to suggest that this is the earlier one. If we follow Lloyd's reasoning, both this song and 'The Blantyre Explosion' (song 27), in expressing the community tragedy in highly personal terms, represent an early stage in the development of industrial balladry, both in character and in function. The personalization ties them close to the ballad-sheet tradition as found in songs of brutal murder and similar such songs, but in the case of the mining disaster ballads the mourning woman is symbolic of the grief of the community at large. I recommend that you read Lloyd's interesting chapter on the subject of industrial song.

'The Blantyre Explosion', being more specific and detailed, typifies a slightly later stage in development than the vague generalized 'Handsome Collier Lad'/'Johnny Seddon'. At a later stage still, coinciding with more widespread and militant trade union activities, the songs lose the passive and fatalistic qualities that inform the earlier ones. Instead they become more statements of policy and discontent.

The song as quoted by Lloyd has an introductory verse which John's does not. On the other hand it does not have the last verse as given here, which is very close to the last verse of 'The Blantyre Explosion'.

The tune given in *Folksong in England* is that commonly used for 'Skibereen', and is different to that given herein.

### 26. The Maid of the Colehill

This was one of the favourite songs of the late Paddy McMahon, the man who introduced me to John Maguire. He liked to hear it sung and, if persuaded to sing himself, would almost invariably sing this song.

All the places mentioned are in the general vicinity of Enniskillen, Co. Fermanagh. Bridge is presumably Maguiresbridge, a small village a few miles from the town. Coleshill (John always says Colehill), named after the Cole family, rich and influential landowners since the Elizabethan Plantation and carrying the title of Earl of Enniskillen among their ranks, is on the edge of a town. It is now taken up by a housing estate.

This song is obviously a close relation to that given the title of 'The Flower of Corby Mill' in SHC, no. 612, which is a fuller version.

### 27. The Blantyre Explosion

On the morning of Monday, 22 October 1877 there was an explosion in shaft number three of the William Dixon and Company coal mine at High Blantyre, about eight miles from Glasgow. Two hundred and thirty-three boys and men were working down that and number two shaft, which was also affected by the spread of gas. Over two hundred of the miners died, making the disaster the greatest mining calamity in Scotland, and second only to a disaster at the Oaks Colliery near Barnsley in 1866 when 340 people lost their lives.

Some idea of the enormity of the anguish caused by the explosion may be gauged from the report in the *Glasgow Herald* the day after which makes the point that 'from almost every household in the locality one or more of the members were among the list of the entombed'.

### 28 Blooming Caroline from Edinburgh Town

This is a fairly well-known song and while fuller versions are to be found (see GG, LXX and JO, 186) this version is complete unto itself. Perhaps it is in the nature of the Ulsterman to cut away all the trimmings and get down to the basic material. The only verse of importance that is missed is the final one where young lovers and parents are warned never to frown on suitors, or sorrow will be the result. It could, on the other hand, be argued that the song is just as good without the moral. You decide!

### 29. The Glasgow Barber
John's brother, Brian, also sings this song. There have been cultural connections between Scotland and Ulster since even before 'the Plantations' of the early seventeenth century. These connections have been consolidated over the years, by commercial and industrial inter-dependence, and in migratory workers like John communication continued. However, it is easy to over-emphasize the similarities between the two societies. Assimilation would not be an easy, smooth affair. This song, although on the surface it is a funny one, gives some indication of underlying frictions. One particularly telling couplet is found in the sixth verse:

> It's before I'd make bargains with the barbers of Scotland,
> I'd rather make bargains with the landlords at home.

When one brings to mind the great antipathy the Irish people in general have towards the landlords the position of the 'Glasgow barber' is not a high one.

### 30. The Bonnie Wee Lassie that Never Said No
At first sight this would seem to be a Scots song and certainly Jeannie Robertson sings a version of it, though not so complete or effective as that given here (Topic Records 12T96). However, so many learned people have insisted that it is an Irish song that I bow to them and grate-fully accept it as such. Certainly the tune used here is an Irish one.

The story line is in the same genre as 'Ratcliffe Highway' (see EFS, p. 85).

## Chapter 6

### 31. Dick Mooney's Daughter
After the famine the small-farmer class in Ireland became very conscious, for various reasons, about the value and importance of land, as this song says: 'That's what they're wanting at this very time'. Of course the land was handed on usually to the male stock but if the calamity, and indeed shame, of no boy-child was visited on the family then perhaps it would be left to a landless nephew, but the female child might get it in the last resort. If the female did have the land then she became extraordinarily desirable; her dowry was great and could overcome almost all 'deficien-cies' in her family background, or in herself.

Michael McDonagh, in his *Irish Life and Character* (Hodder & Stoughton, London, 1898) tells of a farmer who, while admitting that his daughter was 'not very purty', knew that it was possible to 'make her purty with cows'. Dick Mooney is trying to do the same thing in this song. You can judge for yourself whether he succeeded.

For more information about the fascinating subject of marriage style in Ireland I suggest you read C. M. Arensberg and S. T. Kimball *Family and Community in Ireland* (Harvard University Press, Cambridge, Mass., 1948) and any of the work of K. H. Connell. See Glossary for chapter 6, *Matchmaking*.

### 32. Johnny Harte
John is particularly fond of this type of song, what we might call the misalliance songs. One lover, most usually the boy, is poor and the match is frowned upon by the parents of the other, who take various degrees of action. The endings are as various as the details of the story. In 'Johnny Harte' all ends up well with a reconciliation; in 'Blooming Caroline from Edinburgh Town' (song 28) the ending is tragic, and so on.

Sometimes the story seems to be mixed up with the 'Handsome Cabin Boy' type of song. The maid follows her love to sea or war, whence he has gone broken-hearted or at the behest of the girl's parents, e.g. 'The Dandy Apprentice Boy' (song 39).

Other examples of this general story in John's repertoire, as well as the one's mentioned above, are song 33, 'The Lady Heiress and the Farmer's Son', and song 38, 'The Gay Ploughboy'. All have the stamp of ballad-sheets and I have seen one of 'Johnny Harte'. Also see I S B, p. 174, and S H C, no, 106.

### 33. The Lady Heiress and the Farmer's Son
See note for song 32.

### 34. The Wee Tailor from Tyrone
The story of this song only becomes understandable if it is assumed that there is a missing verse. The tailor is loath to marry 'lovely Mollie', in fact he would rather turn to farm labouring or dealing, both considered lowly tasks. Molly follows him, though he doesn't seem to know. It is then that we must assume another verse which develops some relationship between the tailor and the lady, for whom Mollie is working. In the third verse we must accept that it is Mollie, pretending to be the lady of the house – in this way she tricks him into marrying her.

One expects this story to be in folk-songs and folk-tales. However, I have searched in vain for another song or tale version.

## 35. Marrow Bones

This very common song deserves to have been included in Professor Child's definitive compilation of ballads. Perhaps, as Gershon Legman suggests in *The Horn Book* (University Books, New York, 1964), it was a rather extreme prudishness on the part of the scholar that kept it out. This thankfully did not stop it becoming a favourite of the people.

In Scotland it is known as 'The Old Wife of Kelso' and many versions are to be found in the Greig manuscripts, held at Aberdeen University. 'Johnny Sands' (JO, p. 93.) is certainly a relative and is probably the older song. A version from Co. Antrim is to be heard on 'Of Maids and Mistresses', Elektra 137. Another version, recorded from travelling people in Belfast, is on Topic 12T195, vol. 7 of 'Folksongs of Britain'.

## 36. In Praise of John Magee

This is a funny song with a social reality behind it, as do many of the folksongs that poke fun at some element of the man/woman relationship.

Wife-selling was in fact a fairly common practice in the eighteenth and nineteenth centuries. John Ashton in his book *Modern Street Ballads* (Chatto, 1888) notes that there were such sales 'even as lately as last year'. There was a certain amount of ritual about the process. In London the sales often took place in Smithfield market and the women seem to have been led into the auction ring with a halter round their neck or waist; the deal was completed over a drink and included the signing of papers. Prices, according to Ivan Bloch, *Sexual Life in England, Past and Present* (trs. W. H. Forstern, Francis Aldor, London, 1938) seem to have been low.

There are some saving graces for the women however. Sometimes it would seem that the wife sold her husband. Bloch quotes a case in Drogheda at the end of the eighteenth century. It is also suggested by E. P. Thompson that the sale was as often as not a regularizing process of a *de facto* position, i.e. she was often sold to her lover. The penultimate verse of our song would suggest this to be the case in the instance of Mrs Magee: 'Now he being a widow and a neighbour of her own'.

If we regard the wife sales as a form of working-class divorce the concept probably becomes less repugnant to our 'civilized' sensibilities. It was not until 1857 that a divorce could be granted by the courts, but even the radical Matrimonial Causes Act of 1937 did not effectively open them to the working class. They had to wait until the institution of the legal aid provisions in 1949.

I have not had any evidence of the practice being widespread in Ireland. This song, of which I have another version differing only in detail and tune (see FSU, song 12), is the only suggestion I can find that wife-selling happened in Ireland.

*37. The Old Leather Britches*
This ballad-sheet song is probably of the vaudeville tradition. It is common throughout Ireland and I have heard in the Borders of Scotland. John's tune is a particularly good one. See ISB, p. 214. Here the tune given is a different one.

*38. The Gay Ploughboy*
See note for song 32.

*39. The Dandy Apprentice Boy*
See note for song 32 and MISB, p. 18.

*40. The Bonny Irish Boy*
A well-known song throughout these islands. Probably a ballad-sheet. (See JO, p. 162. He has one more verse). The text is close to that sung by O. J. Abbott on Folkways FM4051.

This song offers another reason to the long tally why people have to leave Ireland.

*41. The Factory Girl*
Here is the 'pastourelle' theme brought up to date, but the happy ending that we find in this version of John's is atypical both in general and particular. Usually the blithe young innocent spurns his advances and he mourns.

> It's true I do love her and now she won't have me,
> For her sake I'll wander through valley and dell.
> For her sake I'll wander where no one shall find me
> And I'll die for the sake of my factory girl.

Indeed what else could any self respecting young worthy do? (See FSU, song 19.)

'The Factory Girl', as I say usually with the unhappy ending, is a very common song throughout these islands, carried as it was on a ballad-sheet. Most of the people who have given me songs could sing at least a couple of verses, and the tune has always been close to this one.

I find this song particularly interesting because of the fact that it lends an air of modernity to a very old theme. We might characterize it as a 'transitional song'. The comparatively rural setting of the conversation would tend to suggest that the song comes from that period of industrialization, between cottage production and urbanized steam-driven factories, when factories were situated outside the towns, using water power as the prime-mover. Probably the girl worked in one of the early cotton-spinning establishments built at the end of the eighteenth century.

Given this then, it is not too much to suggest that in this song we can see an attempt by the people involved in that great period of social and economic change called the Industrial Revolution to control their life experiences. They were still steeped in old traditions and methods, but were being bombarded by great changes. The mixture of old and *new* in this song is evidence of their very human attempts to understand the new in terms of the old and secure.

### 42. Erin the Green

This I think is a particularly lovely song and John 'put's it over' very well indeed. It seems to be a great favourite in the area, but not many seem to sing it, probably because it is a very difficult song to sing well.

I have another very close version from Nelly Mullarkey (*FSU*, song 22) though she sings it less freely than John. I have heard that it is also sung in Co. Donegal but Collderry (Coolederry) is a townland in the parish of Magheracloon. I wonder is this from the same pen as 'The Maid of Magheracloon' (see song 6). Certainly the theme and style are very close.

The tune, by the way, owes much to the one that usually carries that great song, 'The Green Linnet'.

### 43. My Charming Edward Boyle

Elsewhere (FSU) I have suggested that this emigration song predates 'the Great Famine' because of, among other reasons, the seeming novelty of emigration. During and after the Famine the people of Ireland lost their innocence in this respect, as millions were spewed out and emigration became institutionalized into the Irish life-style.

Since writing the note for *Folksongs Sung in Ulster* I have heard more about Edward Boyle which, if true, makes the adjective 'charming' very misplaced when applied to him. According to local custom, Edward Boyle came from the Rosslea area and when he got to America he sent for his parents, telling of the great life to be had there. His parents sold up their farm and followed him. According to my informant, 'when he got their wee bit of money for the land, he turned the corner', in other words abandoned them. Surely not the action of a 'charming' young man. My source does not know what happened to the parents, by the way, so that must remain a mystery.

### 44. The Banks of Clady

This is the common 'broken-token ballad' though in most cases the 'broken token' is missing. (However I do have a fragment of a version from Co. Antrim which includes it.) This song is very widely known throughout the British Isles, probably because it was carried on a ballad sheet. I have collected a number of versions throughout Ulster and there are many printed versions available and all are textually very close, though the tunes differ (see songs 5, 45 and 46). See also ISB song 58; SHC, song 693; *FSU*, song 2.

### 45. *The Lass from Glasgow Town*
The first time I heard this song I was lulled into expecting the usual progress of a 'broken-token ballad' (as for instance song 44). Right up to the last verse the story is 'typical' and then in the last verse comes the shock ending. It begins as expected with the girl expressing extreme regret at the reported demise of her lover but then, instead of going on to swear continuing loyalty to her dead man, 'the lass from Glasgow town' transfers her affection to the new love, and that is that.

I must admit I enjoy the change but I feel that this song must have been based on the more usual pattern. It is interesting to muse whether the change is the result of bad memory or a conscious decision. Comparing this with 'Swansea Barracks', as sung by Phil Tanner on vol. 8 of 'Folksongs of Great Britain', Topic 12T196, does not solve the problem. After following basically the same story line as John's song, with of course Swansea Town substituted for Glasgow Town, the last verse is as follows:

> Then on the ground in agonies, this pretty maid did fall.
> Saying I never shall rest, till in my breast there strikes a cannon ball.
> Eight years ago he left me when to Bermuda he was bound,
> And he vowed he would prove faithful to the lass of Swansea Town.

This does not resolve the song even as well as John's. The tune Tanner uses is very close to that used for 'Skibereen' and does not, it is suggested, carry the words as well as the one given here.

The notes to the Topic recording suggest that SHC, no. 612 is a parody of this song. This conclusion seems to be based on the fact that the last lines tend to be the same though the story lines are completely different. The SHC song is much closer, as already noticed, to John's song, 'The Maid of the Colehill', song 26, chapter 5.

### 46. *Smith at Waterloo*
This more than usually specific re-working of the broken token is often called 'The Plains of Waterloo', but should not be confused with the journalistic ballad of the Battle of Waterloo found in GG, LXXXIX and JO, 299. I have collected it from another source in Co. Fermanagh, and Edith Fowke has it from the Ottawa Valley in Canada (see *High Level Ranter's Song and Tune Book*, Galliard and EFDSS, 1972, p. 28). Recorded on Folkways, FM 4051. See also songs 5, 44 and 45 herein. It is now very popular in the English folk-song clubs.

*47. Texas Isle*
This version, and a fairly full one, of 'The Banks of Nile,' though it has been changed in an obvious and direct way, probably in the course of oral transmission. John assures me that this is the way he learned it from his source (Paddy Caddan) which means that either Paddy mislearned it from a ballad-sheet or he got it also in this form. If the latter, which is perhaps more likely, then this mutation has been around since the early years of this century.

The theme of the young girl dressing up in man's attire (or at least expressing the wish to do so) is a common one in the tradition of these islands. Presumably a tradition based on fact – certainly in the archives of an Edinburgh hospital there is detailed the story of one such woman. A poor man was brought into hospital and when he was forced to undress he was seen to be a woman. From there on the story reads like the base for a ballad. She was from a rich family; her love went to war (the Napoleonic Wars, as the incident was written down in the minutes for 1830) and she dressed as a man and followed him; he was killed and she could not go back to her family and so lived as a man.

'The Banks of Nile' song relates to the British army's excursion into Egypt, under the command of Sir Ralph Abercrombie in 1801. They were to expel or subdue the French Army left there by Napoleon. In the decisive battle, which the British won, Abercrombie was wounded and died a week later. See J O, p. 298, G G, xxv. Cf. *EFS*, p. 58.

*48. The Rocks of Giberaltar (fragment)*
This is a fragment of what appears to be a patchwork song, obviously owing a lot to 'The Lowlands of Holland' (G G, cxxxv) which can still be found both in Scotland and England. A fuller version of 'The Rocks of Gibraltar' can be found in G G, lxxxiii and J O. p. 331, but none seem to be very satisfactory as complete songs.

*49. The Old Oak Tree*
This murder ballad has all the marks of a ballad sheet and is known widely throughout Ireland (see *FSU*, no. 15). John's tune is basically the same as the one used in the Galway area, though there it is sung more freely.

*50. The Wee Croppy Tailor*
A fine 'eternal triangle' song known in Ireland and England as well as in America. Known variously as 'The Bold Drover' or 'The Bold Trooper' (see *MB*, p. 6) 'The Groggy Old Tailor' (on Folk Legacy, Record F S E 20).

The unfortunate tailor certainly comes off second best and I'm sure that the punishment he undergoes, though extreme enough, is only symbolic for an even more extreme, though more directly relevant, act of surgery!

### 51. James Magee

Here is a song that highlights the importance that 'land' holds for the Irish country man, an importance that seems to have developed, for various reasons, since the Famine. That the religio-political situation can be used for economic gain will surprise no one who knows what goes on. Indeed there are those, and I would number myself among them, who argue that the basis of the religious bitterness in Ulster is an economic one, and it is not the common people, of whatever side, who gain.

I cannot find any information about James Magee. He was, according to John, 'well schooled', having been educated in Dublin 'for six years'. He understood that James Magee 'was taken the same as John Mitchel' (a leader of the Young Ireland movement). Mitchel had been arrested, found guilty on a charge of sedition and condemned to be transported in May 1848. There is a version of the song in SHC, p. 723.

### 52. The Murder of William Funston

This song is based on fact and indeed John met the son of Funston at a market in Enniskillen. However, I have been unable to come up with anything more concrete.

The story is made fairly clear and such happenings are likely to take place when inter-religious tension is high in this country, so perhaps we can suggest sometime during the 1910s or 1920s as the possible date of this particular incident. At such times each side of the religious divide will tend to think the worst of those on the other side. Such tensions and 'blindness' can be useful to unscrupulous men, of whatever colour. One wonders just how many similar stories will arise out of the present 'troubles'.

On another occasion John sung me this song and he added another verse between 6 and 7 of this recording:

> The case was stated as agitated,
> By the rotten branches of Luther's clan;
> And the cry was hang them, the Yankee fenians,
> That murdered Funston our Orangeman.

Also he replaced the last two lines of verse 8 with the following:

> Ah before concluding our simple verses,
> We hope their freedom will soon be known.

## 53. The Country I Was Born In

This is a good emigration ballad. Here is well expressed the feeling of ambivalence that is part of leaving Ireland's shores. Perhaps the reasons for going have changed a little now but people still go, and they will know what it is to feel torn.

There were good reasons for emigrating in the late nineteenth century when this 'ballad' was written. The pay and prospects at home were bad (verse 1). The landlords were harsh and many people were hungry (verse 4). Nevertheless good times were to be had there and at least you had friends (verse 2). Perhaps some day things would be better (verse 5) and after all 'Old Ireland's the country I was born in'.

Certainly John Maguire knows all about these feelings – he knows what this song is all about.

## 54. Pat O'Donnell

The 1870s and 1880s were disturbed times in Ireland. In 1881 Gladstone had been forced to widen the terms of reference of 'a land act' by a wave of agrarian violence. Many saw this as a victory for Parnell, but many of his allies saw it as a surrender to the government; in America it was viewed as 'the sale of the Land League'. It looked as if Parnell would lose the leadership of the land reform movement but then public attention became preoccupied by the 'Pheonix Park Murders'. At first this event seemed as if it would drive him from public life, but in the end proved to be to his advantage.

On 6 May 1882 the new Lord Lieutenant, Lord Frederick Cavendish, and T. H. Burke, the under-secretary, and the real object of the attack, were assassinated while walking through Pheonix Park Dublin. The 'execution' was carried out by members of 'The Invincibles', a militant underground Republic group based in the capital. James Carey was a member of 'The Invincibles' and was one of those arrested. Carey, in return for a guarantee of safe passage to South Africa, turned Queen's evidence and as a result a number of the organization were convicted and hanged at Kilmainham jail.

Carey was set free, but while on board the Melrose, *en route* for Cape Town, he was shot by Pat O'Donnell. O'Donnell, a native of Co. Donegal was tried and convicted in London, and hanged there on 23 December 1883. The song, which was issued on a ballad-sheet, is a popular one especially in the northern counties of Ireland.

## 55. The Burning of Rosslea

Rosslea (The Grey Wood) has figured much in the various 'troubles' of Irish history. It was an early centre of Orangeism in Co. Fermanagh, and certain to make the area 'sensitive'. It was one of the first centres of the Hibernian movement.

During the 'troubles' of 1921 the R.I.C. barracks in Rosslea was one of the many in 'risky' areas, evacuated at an early stage. When the A-Special's (Mobilized B-Specials) were formed, they took it on themselves to police the area. One of these, Lester, was warned to stop interrogating Catholic children, but when it continued an attempt was made on his life by the IRA and the usual story of escalation began. Lester was wounded and the 'Specials' burned down eight Catholic houses, wounding two in the process. The Monaghan Brigade of the IRA determined to strike back and burn sixteen houses of the Specials, and four NCO's were to be shot. The attack took place on the night of 21 March 1921 and fourteen houses were burned, and the four officers were shot, two fatally. It was at this time that the incident relating to Nixon, that John tells in the text, took place (see chapter 5). The Specials then flowed back into Rosslea and the Catholics once again retreated. The spiral was broken by the captain of the A-Specials who arranged a peace conference of prominent Catholics and Protestants, which was successful. An uneasy peace returned to the area.

As you can see the song follows the story fairly closely. A more detailed account of the incident is to be found in *The Fermanagh Story* by Peader Livingstone, Cumann Seanchais Chlochain, 1969.

# Glossary

Each unusual word or phrase is translated on the first occasion that it occurs and thereafter translation is assumed to be unnecessary.

## Chapter 1

*'til*   John often uses this instead of the word 'to', e.g. 'He walked 'til the window.'

*Recently*   I am honestly not quite sure about this usage and John could not explain. It seems to mean something like 'originally', i.e. 'Her name was Bridget McMahon originally . . .'

*A townland*   An ancient, though still highly relevant, rural administrative unit only used in Ireland. It is the smallest of all these units, e.g. townland, parish, barony and so on. See E. Esytn Evans, *Irish Folk Ways*, Routledge & Kegan Paul, 1957, pp. 27 ff.

*Friends*   This should usually be taken to mean that the individual, or individuals, to whom it relates is a relative of the person being spoken about.

*He's*   Used interchangeably for 'his'.

*I mind*   I remember.

*When they got up middling*   When they had become a little older.

*To ceilidh*   A 'ceilidh' is a gathering of neighbours in one of their houses, usually in the evening. Often the purpose is simply to exchange local gossip. However it might easily, and often does, develop into a session of singing, dancing and story-telling. 'To ceilidh' is to take part in such a gathering. 'Ceilidhers' are those attending 'a ceilidh'. From a Gaelic word.

*An old word*   An old saying.

*Off the pad*   'On the pad' was to be out and about. 'Off the pad' means not out and about and assumes that the individual was usually to be found 'on the pad.'

*Brownchatis*   Bronchitis.

*It bid be* It must be, or it must have been. 'It bid to be' is also used.
*Nor* Than, i.e. 'Older than me'.
*Lowering it and rising it* Description of the traditional style
  decoration of a song.
*It would like to be* It was probably six years ago . . .
*Cooped* Cowped, knocked over, e.g. 'He cooped the basket'.
*The caulkers* Horseshoe nails.
*Churned* The process by which cream is turned into butter, by the use
  of a hand churn. See Evans, op. cit., pp. 93 ff.
*Pratie/purty* Potato. 'Pratai' is the Gaelic word for potato.

## Chapter 2

*Copies* Writing-copy books. It had a phrase printed in 'copper-plate'
  writing at the top of the page. In the space beneath the child
  had to copy the phrase exactly, both words and style.
*Still-tinkers* At one time the stills for making illicit whiskey (poteen)
  were almost exclusively made by travelling people. They made
  new stills or repaired old ones as required. For a discussion of
  poteen-making see chapter 4.
*Childer* Children
*To view* In hunting parlance 'to view' means that a sight has been
  caught of the hunted animal and that a chase will ensue. You
  can see the sense of such a usage in this context.
*Gaelic football* To the uninitiated this game will look like a cross
  between association football and rugby. The fifteen-men teams
  can handle or kick the ball and the goal-posts are rather like
  rugby-posts, only with nets and a goal-keeper, as in association
  football. However the game has no real connections with these,
  being descended from medieval mellays, in which whole
  parishes would be involved. Rules were not laid down until
  1884, when the Gaelic Athletic Association took the game under
  its wing. However it is still a very rough game, not played
  much outside Ireland.
*The Free-State* A term commonly used in Ulster when referring
  to the Irish Republic.
*Hunting* This is not the red-coated, tally-ho!, horseback fox hunting
  of the squires and strong farmers of Ireland. Hunting the hare
  with hounds, usually beagles, is a very favourite pastime with
  the farming community in Ulster. Hunts usually take place
  between early November, when the harvest is finished, and
  March, when cultivation for the new season begins. Farmers
  follow their dogs on foot and the hunt lasts from early morning
  until the sun begins to set.

# Glossary

*The pit*   The ring within which fighting-cocks are 'pitted' for 'the battle'.

*Raygo bags*   Hessian sacks, as used to transport potatoes.

*A piley*   A pilot: a breed of poultry which seem to be great favourites of the cock-fighting fraternity.

*Lay them ready*   Leave them ready.

*The quarter*   The area where the 'pit' is situated.

*Station*   Seems to mean very much the same as 'quarter'.

*Hand him*   Prepare the cock for a 'battle'.

*A differ*   An argument or difference of opinion.

## Chapter 3

*Springer*   A young cow carrying her first calf. Elsewhere called 'a springing heifer'.

*The weight of*   The most of.

*A sally*   The branch of a willow or 'sally-waddle'.

*Chapel*   A Catholic church. In Ulster the distinction is always made between Protestant and Catholic churches by use of this word.

*Chammy*   Chamois.

*Marls*   Marbles.

*A hundred*   A hundredweight.

*A mechal*   The Gaelic word 'meitheal' means a 'gathering of neighbours'. See Daniel Corkery, *The Hidden Ireland*, Gill, 1967, p. 33.

*Earnest*   In Scotland called 'the arls'. In other areas 'fastpenny' or 'Godpenny'.

*Trick of the loops*   A 'game' that still takes in the unsuspecting at fairs and horseraces. A belt is folded and then thrown carelessly on a flat surface. The onlookers are invited to insert a pencil among the folds so that the operator cannot take the belt away while holding the two ends. It looks simple and customers are drawn into wagering both by good odds and by stooges in the crowd, who are allowed to win. It is difficult to put into words how the operator cheats but it is so simple that anyone who plays deserves to lose. I have lost myself many times!

*Wheel of fortune*   Another 'game of chance'. This time the bets are made and paid according to the position of a dart thrown at a revolving wheel. The element of chance is no doubt greater than in 'the Loops' but still Lady Luck is usually helped on her way.

*There inclined to be*   There was likely to be.

*A half-one*   A measure of whiskey. In Ireland a quarter gill.

*Drop calves*   New-born calves.

# Glossary

*Doesn't care about it*   Do not like or approve of.
*A ballad*   A ballad-sheet or broadside.

## Chapter 4

*A ceilidhing house*   This is a house where neighbours regularly gather to ceilidh (see above). Usually just called a ceilidh house.
*Sprees*   A party or ceilidh at which alcoholic drink was available. John explains it himself, later in the chapter.
*A trump*   A jew's harp.
*A melodium*   A melodeon.
*The clear stuff*   Poteen.
*A rebel*   A generic term referring to one who sympathizes, usually actively, with some shade of Irish nationalism.
*Fenians*   The Fenian Brotherhood arose out of the unsuccessful insurrection of the Young Irelanders in 1848, though it was not actually formed until 1858. The aim of this revolutionary society was to overthrow the British rule in Ireland. The leaders argued that nothing could be done by constitutional means and so the organization was essentially a military one. Over the following years the Brotherhood were the prime-movers of disturbances throughout the country (see J. C. Beckett, *The Making of Modern Ireland 1603–1923*, Faber, 1966, pp. 358 ff).
    The name 'Fenian' was derived from the word 'Fianna', the legendary military force led by Finn MacCool, the hero warrior. The name is now applied generically (by Protestants, in a rather deprecating way) to all 'nationalist' sympathizers.
*Stepped*   Steeped.
*Working*   Fermenting.
*The tackle*   The collective name for the 'machinery' used in making poteen.
*Thirty-five bob*   Thirty-five shillings. A 'bob' is the slang term for the shilling. It will be interesting if it dies out under the decimal system.
*The articles*   Another term for 'tackle'.
*Drink*   Poteen.
*Wash*   The brew (of ale) from which 'the drink' is distilled.
*The first shot*   This is the first small amount of 'drink', usually after two or three distillations.
*Singlings*   The liquid gained from the first distillation.
*An old crater*   A phrase inferring sympathy, in this case for an old person.
*The boys with the black peaks*   Policemen.
*Lootin*   A putty made from a mixture of meal flour and water. Used

to seal the join between 'the head' and 'the pot'. See discussion
of poteen-making in chapter 4.

*To red out*   To tidy up.

*The tools*   The same as 'the tackle' and 'the articles'. See above.

*The room*   The good room, the front room, the sitting-room.

*Didn't think a hate of it*   Didn't worry about it.

## Chapter 5

*skim*   What is left after the cream is skimmed off the milk.

*great*   Close friends.

*A cot*   A rather crude, simple, but effective boat, found on the
loughs of Co. Fermanagh. See Evans op. cit., pp. 239 ff.

*The Black and Tans*   By 1919 there had developed in Ireland a state
of war between the British government and the IRA, though
few cared to admit it. The Royal Irish Constabulary, unfitted
both materially and psychologically to wage war, were under
great stress. The Black and Tans, so called because of the
mixture of police and army uniform they had to wear, were
recruited in England to meet these pressures. Along with 'the
Auxiliaries', 'the Tans' formed the spearhead of the government's
attack on the IRA in late 1920 and early 1921. It is argued by
many that, far from helping in the defeat of the IRA, 'the
Tan's' activities heightened the tensions in the country, and
probably the resolve of 'the rebels'.

*The sheough*   In Ireland the word 'ditch' means 'a raised bank'.
Sheough is the name given in the northern counties to the open
ditch alongside the bank.

*Rathes*   Rails.

*A spicket*   An icicle.

*Lucky old crown and anchor*   Poker dice.

*A higgen*   In John's words, 'what they called the boss over you'.

*The road*   The main corridor in the mine from which one gains
access to various coal faces.

*The gauge*   The rail track.

*A piece*   A packed lunch.

*Bureau*   The employment exchange.

*The parish*   The Poor Law administrative unit which supplied a
certain level of social welfare assistance.

*Ballad-singers*   People who sold 'ballads' at fairs, etc., singing the
songs to attract customers.

*The new line*   It is difficult to be precise about the meaning of this
widely used term, but it seems to relate to the main road in the
area.

*A noggin*   A small wooden drink and food vessel, made in a similar
way to barrels. See Evans, op. cit., p. 74.

*A lap of hay*   An armful of hay, folded over the ground and left
back on the ground to dry. See Evans, op. cit., p. 153.

*Never found it*   Not to notice, e.g. 'I never found the time passing'.

*The landing stone*   A large stone, often in a farmyard or outside an
inn, to make alighting from a horse easier.

*The jaundies*   Jaundice.


## Chapter 6

*The matchmaking*   The system whereby parents choose their
children's marriage partners. See K. H. Connell, 'Peasant
Marriage in Ireland', *Economic History Review*, 2nd series, xlv
(1961–2) and C. M. Arensberg and S. T. Kimball, *Family and
Community in Ireland*, Harvard University Press, Cambridge,
Mass., 1948.

*A place*   A farm of one's own.

*A row ris*   An argument began.

*His lone*   On his own.

*The shores*   Covered 'sheoughs'.

*Stirks*   Young cows of fifteen to eighteen months ready to be taken
to the bull for the first time.

*A fiver*   A five-pound note.

# Index of Songs

Note: Where the music is separate from the words, the music page is given in brackets. The relevant page for song notes is given in italics.

185

# Index

Auction mart, 36

Ballad sheets, 37ff
Black and Tans, 60
Blantyre explosion, versions of, 68ff

Ceilidhs, ceilidhing house, 43ff
Clothing, 18, 29ff, 45
Cock-fighting, 18, 24ff
Cot, 58
Courtship, 47; Church's attitude to, 43
Creamery, 57
Cures, jaundy well, 78; poteen as, 54; for sprain, 77ff; for stomach, 77

Dances, 45
Diet, 12ff

Earnest, 33
Employment, 57ff; accident, 76ff, at Blantyre, 65ff; builder's labourer, 67; coal mines, 65ff; in England, 76ff; leaving Scotland, 74; lodging conditions, 63; navvying, 62ff; in north of Scotland, 62ff; road mending, 74ff

Fairs, 32ff; hiring, 32ff
Family, brothers and sisters, 8ff; children, 94ff; father, 2; mother, 2; uncle and aunt, 8

Farming, 27ff; changes in methods, 93ff; children's work, 31; harvest, 31ff; help from neighbours, 31, 93ff; horse plough, 94; last sheaf, 32; problems of own farm, 92ff; purchase of own farm, 79ff; women's work, 28ff

Gaelic football, 19ff
General strike, 66ff
Ghost, 4ff

Houses, 23ff
Hunting songs, 23ff

IRA, 61ff

Lies, pennyworth of, 75ff
Lough Ooney, 57ff

Marriage, 79ff; ending of, 90; honeymoon, 92; match making, 80ff; wedding party, 92; why some do not undertake, 81ff
Mining accidents, 65ff
Molly Maguires, 21ff
Motor cars, lack of, 22
Murder of Flannigan, 38ff
Music and musical instruments, 45ff

Nicknames, 30

# Index

Potatoes, Aran Victor, 29;
Champion, 13, 29; Flounder,
29; failure of, 30ff; Kerr's
Pink, 13, 29; machine spraying,
29ff; spraying, 29ff
Poteen, 16; church's attitude, 50,
52ff; as cure, 54; effects, 50;
legal aspects, 50ff; making,
49ff

Retirement, 95
Rosslea, burning of, 61ff

School, 14ff
Settling at home, 78
Sheough, 60
Skittles, 19ff
Songs, authorship, 17ff, 38;

brother's and sister's, 8;
Catholic and Protestant, 76;
father's, 2; learning, 9ff, 47,
58, 64, 70, 71, 72, 85-6; making
his own, 21ff; mother's, 6;
party, 22; singing session, 85ff;
singing in unison, 8ff
Spade mills, 28ff
Spades, 27ff
Street musicians, 74ff

'The Troubled Times', 60ff
Trick o' the Loops, 33

Volunteers, 61

Wakes, 54ff
Willie the Wisp, 41ff